SHAEMAS O'SHEEL

Antigone and Selected Poems

SHAEMAS O'SHEEL

Shaemas O'Sheel
ANTIGONE *and* SELECTED POEMS

Edited by Annette K. O'Sheel
With an Appreciation by A. M. Sullivan

PHILADELPHIA · UNIVERSITY OF PENNSYLVANIA PRESS

A Note

It has been suggested that I explain why I have chosen for republication only the last book of poems—the Selected Verse—of Shaemas O'Sheel together with his version of the *Antigone* of Sophokles, omitting his earlier works published in *The Blossomy Bough* and *The Light Feet of Goats*.

The "Why" of the Selected Verse presented as *Jealous of Dead Leaves* was set out by the poet himself in the book published in 1928 which is here reprinted. Reading his explanation makes clear why I have chosen to be guided by his own words that "this selection represents the best I am capable of as a maker of verses."

Again, the reason for the writing of *Antigone* is plainly stated by Mr. O'Sheel in its foreword where he also says: "This book is a small contribution to the work of restoring some of the greatest works of all literature to our own living times."

Of the remaining seven verses included in this volume and not previously published in book form, six were chosen as a result of inquiry over the years about a line or phrase which lay in others' memories; the last one, "Replying To Many Kind Friends," because it indicates the passing of the poet on his immersion into world currents and reveals, too, the humor which was a sparkling facet of his personality.

Annette K. O'Sheel

"HE WENT FORTH TO BATTLE . . ."

In Memoriam Shaemas O'Sheel

By A. M. Sullivan

Shaemas O'Sheel died on April 2, 1954, at the age of sixty-eight. Poet, tractarian, political adventurer, social philosopher, and above all, lover of Irish cultural tradition, Shaemas is forever endeared to Irish literary enthusiasts for two great poems that are in all standard anthologies, "They Went Forth to Battle But They Always Fell," and "He Whom a Dream Hath Possessed." His "Battle of Brooklyn," an account of the losing battle for the Americans in which General John Sullivan participated, was read before the assembled members of the American Irish Historical Society nearly thirty years ago. Shaemas, who was gifted with a superb reading voice, often quoted other poets at the society meetings.

Shaemas O'Sheel's career in literature and politics was stormy, and not often rewarding to him. He favored the underdog, the lost cause, and the minority, and at times with more fervor than discretion. Yet, at the Memorial Services held on May 4, 1954, at the Master Institute on West 103 Street in New York City, a host of admirers and mourners gathered in harmony to do him honor, despite contrary to conflicting personal views. Principally they came to pay homage to the poet, the artist, the humanitarian. The writer of these notes served as chairman of the occasion at the invitation of Annette O'Sheel, his widow. Among those present were the Hon. Claude G. Bowers, former Ambassador to Spain and later to Chile, the biographer of Jefferson and author of *The Tragic*

Era; Alfred Kreymborg, poet and past president of the Poetry Society of America; James McGurrin, president general of the American-Irish Historical Society; Helene Mullins, lyric poet and novelist; Eileen Curran, Irish-born folklore authority and actress; Samuel A. De Witt, poet, business man and one-time Socialist Assemblyman in the New York State legislature; Hon. James Garrett Wallace, distinguished New York jurist; David Ross, poet and radio celebrity.

During the program the chairman called Messrs. Kreymborg, De Witt, McGurrin, and Bowers for comments, which varied from frank appraisals to unstinted praise. Many of the anecdotes, recalled with mixed humor and regret, depicted Shaemas as the voluble dissenter at the Poetry Society meetings during its early years, and later as a stalwart champion of the Men of Easter Week, when to voice an approval of the rebels wasn't the popular thing to do in polite society. David Ross read selections from *Jealous of Dead Leaves,* which was published in 1928 and contained many of the poems from *The Blossomy Bough* and *The Light Feet of Goats.* The chairman read O'Sheel's poem "Replying to the Many Kind Friends Who Ask Me if I No Longer Write Poetry." Letters of condolence were read from Sean O'Casey and Van Wyck Brooks.

Shaemas O'Sheel, born James Shields, never saw Ireland but gaelicized his name as evidence of his devotion to a romantic and spiritual ideal. He was at work on a history of the Irish Race in America when death intervened. The completed chapters reveal that he spent several years in research, and indicate great care as well as superb craftsmanship in writing. Shaemas the poet was part of the lyric awakening in America. *Blossomy Bough,* his first book, was published in 1911, and while he was conformist in poetic techniques he was always an adventurer in ideas. He won immediate acclaim, and published *The Light Feet of Goats* in 1915, which also received wide praise from the critics, even though the Free Verse and Imagist movement was gathering momentum. However, he had an itch for the political arena, and the lyric candle dimmed amidst the dust of dialectics. Shaemas was a skilled pleader for minority rights. He was a prolific correspondent with anyone about most anything, pro or con. He debated with zeal but without rancor.

Much of this side of Shaemas is recalled in a talk given by Claude Bowers, who had served in the legislative chambers at Washington when Claude and Shaemas were staff employees of Indiana and New York senators.

Years ago, fresh from the acclaim that had greeted his published poems, Shaemas O'Sheel appeared in Washington as a member of the staff of Senator O'Gorman. I was fairly familiar with some of his poems, and somehow I had the impression that he was a poet of tradition patterned after the Bohemians of Montmartre. I was a bit startled to find him meticulously correct in attire. He might have passed as an exhibit from Saville Row. And his hair was neither long nor ragged. I was to find that Yeats, not Villon, was his model.

Talking with him about Ireland, one was transported to the green isle, and could smell the smoke of the peat fires in the cabins, and hear the murmur of the Shannon, and feel the charms of Killarney, and glimpse the glistening green that stretched from Galway to the Hill of Howth. I never tired of hearing him talk with a touch of passion of the history, the traditions, and the poetry of the race.

I thought at the time it was unfortunate that he had left the literary atmosphere and companionship of New York for Washington. It transported him from poetry to political polemics; and responding to the instinct of the race, he was almost immediately involved in the bitter controversies of the years just before we entered the First World War. The poet disappeared in the pamphleteer. He became obsessed with the great debate. Like Bryan and LaFollette he thought the arming of merchant vessels and the travel of Americans on the vessels of warring nations an invitation to war. It is not generally known that the historic McLemore Resolution was written by Shaemas. . . .

He was equally at home in the drawing room, the literary tea or a melee like those of Donnybrook Fair. One of his endearing qualities was that he could savagely attack a friend's point of view without in the least diminishing his personal regard for the friend. He would have made a fine advocate but a poor judge, for nature would have made him a partisan on the bench. In those early tempestuous days of his flaming youth one often see-sawed between an impulse to lash him or embrace him. He was not a figment of the fancy; he was real; he was an individual; he was a personality. In a moment of mental aberration he once sought a congressional nomination and he was refused it for the good of his soul. In a party caucus he would have been like a bull in a china shop. He lacked the flexibility of a successful politician. He would not have compromised on principle for the sake of harmony, for his convictions were as unyielding as the rock of Gibraltar.

Looking down the long corridor of the years, lined with friends of other days, I find no figure more colorful, with more sparkle and charm than that of Shaemas O'Sheel. He lives in the memory of all who knew him and loved him.

To return to the first person, my acquaintance with Shaemas occurred early in the twenties, and blossomed into friendship in the thirties, when he organized the Irish cultural organization, The Companions of Brendan. I succeeded him as president about 1935. Shaemas and I disagreed on many things, often political, less frequently poetical, but never on anything dealing with the arts, literature and language of the Irish people.

Contents

2. Poems, 1924-1932

3. *Antigone*

1. Jealous of Dead Leaves

> ". . . . . let us be
> Jealous of dead leaves
> in the bay-wreath crown"
> KEATS

WHY . . .

As long ago as 1918 it was suggested that I should prepare a book to consist of selections from *The Blossomy Bough* and *The Light Feet of Goats*. Two small editions of the former, published in 1911 and 1912, and one of the latter, published in 1915, had been exhausted.

Then began an examination of conscience, a humble weighing and judging, a minute line by line consideration, a process of revision and elimination, which has gone on from time to time. Although the 127 things included in those earlier volumes were a selection from a larger number which had appeared in magazines and newspapers, it was quickly evident that many of them did not deserve republication and that even the better among them exhibited many faults. Maturing judgment has, down the years, cast out more and more of them, and wrought considerable changes in many of the forty-two here retained; three of these, indeed, have been completely rewritten.

I should like to make this the occasion for setting forth

certain ideas about verse and poetry, schools and tend-encies, æsthetic theories and technical problems; but my advisors and publishers unanimously counsel against it. I must be content to note that in the first lyric rapture of youth, I literally flowed verse as naturally as a spring flows water, and I called it poetry; but now poetry has become to me a high and distant goal, and a poem seems to me a kind of miracle not often accomplished. I could not bear to be judged by the faulty work of my uncritical literary adolescence, and the better things in my earlier volumes, having, once created, a sort of life and character of their own, seemed entitled to my labors to bring them to such perfection as I am capable of. It is not for me to say whether any of them now approaches poetry; but I hope that those who were kind enough to like them in their earlier forms will like them better now, and that those to whom they are new will find among them some things worthy of a place in the great body of lyric verse which is the heart's cry in the clutch of sorrow and the heart's song in the gladness of life and love.

SHAEMAS O'SHEEL

THIS IS OUR DOOM

A slender sheaf—straw, straw and a few poppies,
For all the labor of our days.
A few dreams, dreams troubled and elusive,
Though the nights are long.
Ashes, our hearts at last a handful of ashes,
And yet their flames
Light such a little space in the dusk of Time.

This is the doom of those whose desire is unbounded,
To feel in the dark
The wall insurmountable,
To hear beyond hearing the song that shall never be heard,
To see beyond seeing the picture that shall not be painted;
To sense forever
In wind and water,
In wood and meadow,
In city and solitude,
More than the heart can hold or the mind encompass.
This is our doom, we weavers of Time's pale garlands,
To seek forever and find not the Rood and the Rose,
The Lips and the Grail that trouble our fevered dreams.

THEY WENT FORTH TO BATTLE BUT THEY ALWAYS FELL

They went forth to battle but they always fell.
Something they saw above the sullen shields.
Nobly they fought and bravely, but not well,
And sank heart-wounded by a subtle spell.
They knew not fear that to the foeman yields,
They were not weak, as one who vainly wields
A faltering weapon; yet the old tales tell
How on the hard-fought field they always fell.

It was a secret music that they heard,
The murmurous voice of pity and of peace,
And that which pierced the heart was but a word,
Though the white breast was red-lipped where the sword
Pressed a fierce cruel kiss and did not cease
Till its hot thirst was surfeited. Ah these
By an unwarlike troubling doubt were stirred,
And died for hearing what no foeman heard.

They went forth to battle but they always fell.
Their might was not the might of lifted spears.
Over the battle-clamor came a spell
Of troubling music, and they fought not well.
Their wreaths are willows and their tribute, tears.
Their names are old sad stories in men's ears.
Yet they will scatter the red hordes of Hell,
Who went to battle forth and always fell.

THE FIELD OF DUST

This is the field of dust.
Spear-flash and sword-thrust
Wages the battle here,
Aye, and long must!
How does this field appear?
Once 'twas a flowery place—
Gone now its vernal grace,
Trampled by steeds a-race,
Littered with sword and mace,
Wreckage and rust.
Timidly there and here
Virginal vales appear,
But the tense atmosphere
Darkens with dust.

Who is it, foul of face,
Leads a foul host apace
Into this frightened place?
Lo, he is strong!
All the winds shrink and flee,
Curdles the earth, yet see,
They own his majesty,
Loathsome and strong.
Lo, he is known too well,
He is the Khan of Hell,
Regent is he of Wrong,
Lord of this reeling throng,
Reeling and whirling long,
Savage and fell.
Leads he this host obscene,
Miring the living green,

Leaving no waters clean,
Chanting a spell
Whereat the Heavens flame
Scarlet with wordless shame
And all things of fair fame
Echo of Hell.
Delicate things they dash
Doomward, fair temples crash
Terribly, and their lash
Cuts to the bone.
Woe to all things that grow
Upward, and wail and woe
Unto the fair, follow
That host alone.
Ah that the green and fair
Valleys of anywhere
Must know and must,
Such a dark armament
Fouling the firmament,
Making a flowery zone
Dark field of dust.

Spear-flash and sword-thrust
Wages the battle here,
Aye, and long must.
See what bright wings appear
Over the dust!

Who is it, glad with grace,
Morning upon his face,
Swifter than light apace
Pierces the dark,
Strikes to his mark,

22

Glorifies all the place,
Laying the demons stark?
Hark to his clarion, hark—
Sunlight made audible,
Glad with a golden spell,
Golden with grace!
White all his warriors are,
Each spear a piercing star,
Lending a light to war,
And every face
Blends wrath and pity so
Scarce need they strike a blow.
Fair things that used to grow
In this sad place
Look up and glorify
Once more an aureate sky,
And the dread demons fly
Shrieking and fall and die
Stricken apace.
Surely his name is known
Close to the Infinite Throne,
Sure it must spell
Strength of the Living God—
Hail, Mich-a-el!

Spear-flash and sword-thrust
Wages the battle here,
Aye, and long must.

What is the field of dust?
What are the hosts that here
Robed with red wrath appear,
Hot with war-lust,

Dark mace and starry spear
Splint'ring in mad career,
Clouding a world so fair
With their grim gust?
Ah, not from Heaven or Hell
Host they who wage so well:
Lucifer, Mich-a-el
Are not their names.
Their strength no miracle
Of power Celestial
Nor of the Flames.
And the broad battle-place
Where they meet face to face
Bruiting their claims,
Is no terrestrial strand,
No astrologic land:
I am those valleys, and
I am their names.

I am the field of dust,
I who am body and soul.
I am the muster-roll
Of all the demons foul,
I am the splendid whole
Legion whose spears extol
God, whose sword-thrust
Gilds the dark dust.
Here does the battle roll
Endless, and must.
I am the Khan of Hell,
Regent am I of Wrong,
I am God's angel strong,
I, Mich-a-el.

Out of the deeps of me
Throng the red cavalry
And the white angels, see,
In my soul dwell.
Naught can assail me, naught
Cause the red ruin wrought
But my own lust,
And I can trust
Naught but my God-hood, naught.
My own the rage outpoured,
I am the spear and sword,
I am the Fiend and Lord,
I am the dust.

Spear-flash and sword-thrust
Rages the battle here,
Aye, and long must.

CONSCIENCE

For all our whipped and goaded ecstasies,
Our passionate forgettings, we remember—
Amid the mirth and music we remember—
How One is waiting with an ultimate question
Before the inviolable gates of God.

THE PITILESSNESS OF DESIRE

No. I have done. Implacable desire,
Cease, cease!
No more the urgent ways, no more, I tire—
I who went forth mantled with morning fire
Pray now surcease
And peace—peace.

O passionate terrible futile fierce desire,
Imperative and vain,
Blow not again
Your irresistible trumpet, and your lyre
Sound not again.
There is no magic in your martial choir
Now, only pain.

A young soul, sure of wonder, hot blood in the heart,
Limbs of the leaping goat—all these I had,
And spurned a myriad summits gained, to start
Down through new vales to newer heights apart,
And I was glad
Of every peril, I was insatiably mad
For more—more—knowledge, wisdom, passion, art!

But now release
Your broken bondsman from his broken bond.
What is beyond
This and the next horizon and beyond
The last horizon, could not give me peace:
That I have learned at last, and therefore cease
The bloody goad and the illusory wand.

My life's a burning arrow shot in the dark,
Fearfully arching heaven to find no mark.
Must it be always warfare, never peace?
Nay then I ground my arms, I will not hark
The old command. I watch a dying fire,
I turn to the calm hills, to the rooted trees.
Yet—that mad vision, beckoning beyond these!
O protean pitiless perilous dread desire,
Cease, cease!

OUTWORN

Oh unassuageable thirst, oh wordless hunger,
   And all that is the grey of dying hours,
      Dead things that wear the semblance of desires
Long since betrayed and virginal no longer,
   Feverish with the futile lust of powers
      That once lit all the world with morning fires!

Not as of old your tremulous whispering fingers,
   Autumnal poplars, move across my soul
      Soothing it like white hands upon the brow.
It is a bitter thing that memory lingers,
   It is a bitter thing that seasons roll,
      But oh, most bitter the inexorable Now!

Not as of old O grey of dying hours,
   O green O gold O rose that die to grey,
      Not as of old are you the ultimate glory,
The perfect bloom of light. Rather, sad flowers
   Languishing for their lady torn away
      From her fair garden in some tragic story.

Beneath unpitying clouds, over dull waters,
   Defeated flags irreparably torn
      Droop from the sad walls of the hollow West.
Weary with strife are the sons of men, and the daughters
   Weary with passionate waiting, and outworn
      Is all the impulsive rapture of the quest.

Gold, and the color of rose, and the green of the world
   Only a mask to hide the ashen face
      Of Death, the master of Time's pageantry!

Oh beautiful ones, a pitiless net is curled
    Under the rushes, under the revels' pace:
        This night ends all, no dawn will ever be.

Dawn but a dream—and waking we press once more
    Westward, upon the solitary path
        That leads through vistaed sunset into night.
Hoping for peace we meet our doom of war,
    Loving, we bow to this implacable wrath.
        Emptied of faith at last, emptied of might,

We are grey phantoms of the dying hours,
    Doomed things, wearily passing. O fair face,
        Do you not bear one memory of the morn?
What is the light upon your brow—what flowers
    Bloom in your hand? I see the ineffable grace
        Of drooping petals, of fading days forlorn.

OUR LITTLE DAYS

Our days are like drops of water that drip perhaps from
    a fern-frond
Into a quiet pool. Our immemorial days
Drop drop one by one into the Pool of Time.
Little ripples rise, hope and joy and passion,
Little ripples rise, fretting the pool's surface,
Little ripples rise and flow and ebb and are gone,
And quiet comes and peace comes and broods on the Pool
    of Time.

THE LIGHT FEET OF GOATS

Up from lone peak to peak of thought if we leap,
From height to lonelier visionary height,
As goats light-footed leap along windy crags,
It is our dreams that muscle us, steady the eye,
Give us the sure foot and the exultant heart.
Dreams are the light feet of goats on the crags of Time.

HE WHOM A DREAM HATH POSSESSED

He whom a dream hath possessed knoweth no more of
    doubting,
For mist and the blowing of winds and the mouthing of
    words he scorns.
No sinuous speech and smooth he hears, but a knightly
    shouting,
And never comes darkness down, yet he greeteth a million
    morns.

He whom a dream hath possessed knoweth no more of
    roaming.
All roads and the flowing of waves and the speediest flight
    he knows,
But wherever his feet are set his soul is forever homing,
And going he comes, and coming he heareth a call and goes.

He whom a dream hath possessed knoweth no more of
    sorrow.
At death and the dropping of leaves and the fading of
    suns he smiles,
For a dream remembers no past and takes no thought of
    a morrow,
And staunch amid seas of doom a dream sets the ultimate
    isles.

He whom a dream hath possessed treads the impalpable
    marches.
From the dust of the day's long road he leaps to a laugh-
    ing star,
And the ruin of worlds that fall he views from eternal
    arches,
And rides God's battlefield in a flashing and golden car.

TRUTH AND PASSION

(For Anne)

There is a fire God holds in His naked hands.
Above the clouds, above the unquiet clouds
We see it as a star and call it Truth.
I think that these blown flames of our gusty passions,
That feed on Beauty and have Love for their brightness,
Are wandering sparks of that eternal fire.
They will abide. Our joys are mayflies, dying
After a feeble flutter of wings. Our hopes
Fade fast as Winter twilights, and our firm
Fixed purposes are lamps that flicker and fail.
But these shall burn, outlasting the clinkered stars,
When tired God blows out the lights of Time.

THE LOVER PRAISES HIS LADY'S BRIGHT BEAUTY

Some night I think if you should walk with me
Where the tall trees like ferns on the ocean's floor
Sway slowly in the blue deeps of the moon's flood,
I would put up my hands through that impalpable sea
And tear a branch of stars from the sky, as once I tore
A branch of apple blossoms for you in an April wood.

And I would bend the dewy branch of stars about your
    little head
Till they flamed with pride to be as blossoms amid your
    hair,
But I would laugh to see them so pale, being near your
    eyes.
I would say to you "Love, the Immortals are hovering
    about your head,
They laugh at the dimness of stars in the luminous night
    of your hair."
I would toss that weeping branch back to the mournful
    skies.

THE LOVER SCORNS ALL WOMEN BUT HIS LADY

Were all the women of the world to come
And droop their languorous hair about my heart,
They could not hold it in those nets so fine,
And pleading with lips lyrical or dumb,
Pleading with excess of all amorous art,
They could not win the kisses that are thine.

If Helen came, her white limbs hung with gold,
And Deirdre with dim visionary eyes,
And Grania, flame-haired, fiery with command;
If Hero came—reluctant once of old—
And she who all too long with Romeo lies,
And she who led Dante heavenward by the hand,

They could not make me fain of their fain lips
Nor lure me to the languor of warm breasts
With any soft compulsion of white arms,
And delicate dim touch of finger tips
And smouldering eyes where passion leaps and rests
Would leave me cold and lose the name of charms.

Nay, Solomon's Love and Anthony's Desire,
Heloise and frail Francesca, and their queen
Immortal Aphrodite, whom I praise,
Naked before me could not touch with fire
The calm pulse of my blood, for I have seen
Beauty within thy beauty for all days.

LOVE WILL OUTBLOOM THE WORLD

Oh more than ever and more than I can tell
I love you, and my love grows evermore,
As the wave widens to the waiting shore
From the small wound wherein the pebble fell.
Such way of love beyond all ways is well,
Since the heart does not burn to a sad core
With its first flaming, but forevermore
Grows more intense with love than I can tell.

Think O Belovéd to what nameless glory
This flower must grow which blossomed first so fair,
For surely wakened never anywhere
So proud a Rose of Love, in deed or story.
It will outbloom this withering clod the world,
Rooted in God and never to be furled.

THE LOVER THINKS OF HIS LADY IN A GLEN

I loitered in a little glen.
A bird was there and nothing else
Except the waters wandering by.
Whitely they fell and wandered by,
A bird flew over, nothing else
Save I, within the lonely glen.

I called upon the waters then
To sing your name; and nothing else
Should be the bird's melodious cry.
The waters fell and wandered by,
A droning music, nothing else.
A bird song wavered through the glen.

And since the waters would not cry
Your name of names and nothing else,
Nor the bird sing it through the glen,
I breathed it through the leafy glen.
Then the hushed air began to pulse,
And joyous winds to wander by.

THE LOVER BIDS ALL PASSIONATE WOMEN MOURN

Mourn with red lips, pale women who wander alone,
Having each a sorrow too great for another to share,
Deirdre whose fate was saddest because you were most
     fair,
Finavar, doomed for your pride to carry a heart of stone,
And all who were broken because of your loveliness,
Mourn with dishevelled hair, for you understand
The heart of a lover, you know that its bitter distress
If love should fail, is more than the grief of a land
For its strong spear-bearing sons who have met defeat.
Mourn for I tell you my Love who is passing sweet
As berries in Autumn, and fair as a blossomy bough,
And proud with a pride like yours, pale sorrowful ones,
Has taken her thoughts from me and broken her vow,
And the world is a terrible crumbling of moons and of suns.
Mourn with dim eyes, O sad and beautiful ones.

THE BITTERNESS OF LOVE

As I went through the rustling grasses
Over the long low dune,
I saw on the sands two lovers,
And I saw the waves and the moon.

And I heard the unaltering murmur
Of the sea, and a wind that stirred,
And I heard the lovers breathing
Many a passionate word.

And because I too am a lover
And my love is far from me,
I hated the two on the sands there,
And the moon and the wind and the sea.

WHEN SHE CAME NOT

I thought I heard her when the wind would pass
Down through the pine trees and the tangled grass,
I thought I heard her tremulously near
When no sound was.
I thought I heard her little feet
Over the wave-washed pebbles beat
And that I need but lift mine eyes
And see her there without surprise.
I thought, alas!
That she was tremulously near
When no sound was,
And raised my head and threw my arms apart.
    But she
Was nowhere 'twixt the forest and the sea.

HER WAY WITH MY DREAMS

The wind stirs the tangle of her tresses
    where she stands.
She stoops and gathers in rose-pale hands
A myriad grains of the drifting sands.

Musing, she sifts them through fingers slim:
The wind whirls them seaward, a current dim.
They are soon forgotten, as any whim.

She gathered my dreams as the drifting sands,
Gently, as one who understands:
She scattered them with rose-white hands.

THE SEEKER OF ROSES GOES ASTRAY

Where is the valley of poppies?
I have lost my way.
I sought the valley of roses.

But I went astray.
I shall never find the roses.
I want the poppies today.

Where is the valley of clover?
I am wandering.
None will know me a lover,

And there's peace for everything
In the white valley of clover.
I shall not sing.

Ah, some still vale and wordless, anyone!
My quest was a rose-quest,
But I've lost them, that is done.

Maybe I found and bruised them,
Is that what you say?
Maybe—I will not tell.

But I am astray:
Where are the poppies, the clover?
Show me some way!

THE LOVER ENVIES AN OLD MAN

I envy the feeble old man
Dozing there in the sun.
When all you can do is done
And life is a shattered plan,
What is there better than
Dozing in the sun?

I could grow very still
Like an old stone on a hill
And content me with the one
Thing that is ever kind,
The tolerant sun.
I could grow deaf and blind
And never hear her voice
Nor dream I could rejoice
With her in any place.
I could forget her face,
Forget, and have done.
Because when we are tired,
Very, very tired,
And cannot again be fired
By any hope,
The sun is so comforting!
A little bird under the wing
Nestling, is not so warm.
Give me only the scope
Of an old chair
Out in the air,
Let me rest there,
Moving not,
Loving not,
Only dozing my days till my days be done,
Under the sun.

44

MYSELF, NOT GALAHAD

Before the picture of an armored knight
She placed a candle with a little light,
A tapered candle with a steady flame
That put a glow of gold about the name
Galahad. "It is your candle" was her word,
And first I wondered, then my youth was stirred
To a resolve as fine as this her thought,
To be her knight in all things, and in naught
Less worthy of her than that storied knight,
Puissant and pure above my candle's light.

How long before I learned that youth is frail
When in the lonely questing of the Grail
Immediate sweet cups are offered him?
How long before I knew that dreams can dim,
And only a tenuous thread of faith remain
The wanderer's guide through ways of sin and pain?
How long before my knightly crest sunk low?
Yet for the whole adventure I can show
At last the only guerdon that I sought,
My Love's own love; because it seemed as naught
To her that I had mingled good and bad.
It is myself she loves, not Galahad,
And when disarmed I came to her again,
She kissed me. There is no more sin or pain.

THE LOVER IS SURE OF LOVE

When I went hushed and lonely
Where violets were blue
And little wood-anemones
Were white, I thought of you.

And when amid white daisies
I lay on fragrant grass,
With carefree comrades singing
To help the twilight pass—-

Although my head was pillowed
On gay Camilla's arm,
Her small hand warm within my own
And over me her charm,

Although I twined pale blossoms
Into her red-gold hair,
And saw her eyes above me bent
And saw that they were fair—

My heart, O my Belovéd,
Was silent with a dream,
And through the twilight of my soul
There came a vibrant gleam:

And as the stars flamed whitely
Down deepening seas of blue,
My being broke to flame-like love
And star-like thoughts of you.

IN TIME OF FAILURE THE LOVER TAKES
COMFORT IN LOVE

Though chosen fellows prove but fools
And brothers sworn betray my trust
And topple my towers to the dust
And break my sword and dull my tools,

Though all my labor is in vain,
My ev'ry plan a bubble blown,
My ev'ry hope a phantom flown,
My sole reward the coin of pain—

And though the crown I thought to make
For you, and all I thought to win
Of jewelled delights to set therein
With loving labor for your sake

Must now be numbered with the grey
Pale phantoms that forevermore
Await upon life's farther shore
The word that God forgets to say—

What matter, Love? I seem to wake
From some hot frenzy of a dream,
And all I did therein I deem
But faulty service for your sake.

And here in the calm hush of night,
With many quiet stars above,
I weave a robe of perfect love
From cloth of dark and threads of light,

I weave a robe of perfect love
From all the beauty of the night,
And you will wear it in despite
All sorrow, and be glad thereof.

ON AN APRIL EVE

My lover gave three kisses,
He kissed me thrice when we met,
And each kiss lingers with me
Like music I cannot forget.
There are duties that wait my doing
And the moments are passing—yet—
My lover gave three kisses
To me, to me when we met.

Like the winds of the Spring is my lover,
Impetuous, fain of delight.
Quickly he drew me to him
And he held me close in his might:
He called me as fair as the blossoms
That are making the branches bright.

He called me as fair as the blossoms,
But I know when he comes tonight
He will say there's no starry beauty
Like my own eye's little light—
He will tell me that when he holds me
Close to his heart tonight.

Oh my cheeks and my throat he kindled
With kisses today, but my mouth
Was locked like the lips of the meadow
In the length of the Winter's drouth.
Tonight he will lure and compel me
With the warmth of the winds of the South,
I shall throw back my head, and my lover
Will waken the Spring on my mouth.

COLD BEAUTY

Cold lips to kiss not but obey,
Cold eyes that grant no passion sway,
This is her beauty in the day.

Ah but I know how fiercely bright
When bared to one dear lover's sight
Her beauty flames and burns at night!

AN ISLE OF DREAMS

Lone, in a sea of many currents, a fair island.
The waters rage and the winds bear sudden terrors.
Winds and waters grow calm at the shores of the island.

Grey, as a glen ere the dawn, dream-laden, grey—
Green terrible deeps in the waters, and on the winds
Red lightning—but over the island all things are grey.

Immortal sunset saddens evermore
Under the drooping sky ; but like a song
Unbreathed, eternal dawn hovers on Heaven's shore.

Flowers like dear remembered words are there,
And vales like dearer memoried silences.
Old glances of loved eyes are the blue lakes there.

Only upon the secret island, the grey isle of dreams,
Are beauty, freedom, peace : there only heart's content.
Wings are folded at last in still places on the isle of
    dreams.

ISADORA

I

The islands dawn out of the mist, the blue
Islands dawn out of the sea, the silver
Waves break upon saffron sands, and flashing,
The feet of laughing girls scatter the gleaming
Dew, scatter the dewdrops from the purple
Hyacinths, dancing waywardly to the distant
Clear winding of Poseidon's twisted conch.

Ah, Hellas, Hellas, dawn of this troubled human
Dream, lift up, lift up your hyacinthine
Headlands. All your honey colored, honey
Laden meadows murmur again with music,
Thin reedy notes startle once more your leafy
Glades where rushy pools caress the pallor
Of maiden limbs, and mossy couches know the
Sweet pains of maiden love. The long sun-dappled
Long silent aisles beneath the oak trees echo
The lute of Orpheus; upon the ancient
Hills, upon the little hills the ancient
Olives lean and listen; and the lonely
Midnights of windy mountains know the argent
Piping of shepherds amorous of the stars.

II

O Proserpine awaken,
Your poppied slumber shaken
By these swift feet that flash across the centuries and the
    seas.
O goddess glad, renascent,

52

Trouble our hearts complacent,
Trouble us with the wonder of her passionate ecstasies.

See, garlanded and gracious,
From realms serene and spacious,
A grave and ancient rapture she has brought our troubled
    times.
Bearer of mystic treasures,
With magic in her measures,
She comes, her light steps lyric and her white feet shod
    with rhymes.

III

Towers dawn suddenly out of the mist, eager
Towers reach up, seizing the dawn, impatient
Towers that fretted all the night, resenting
The hand of darkness soothing, the hand of silence,
They snatch the dawn, bending it down, breaking
Its roseate loveliness, breaking its fragile
Stillness, suddenly clamorous with a million
Voices. Old Poseidon's horn not heard here,
Nor the half-dreamy songs of dancing girls, nor
Lute notes and argent pipings. From the waters
Jubilant whistles piercing the sunlight, deep-toned
Horns throbbing, throbbing into the blood. Here
Up from the granite canyons, up from the steel-ribbed
Furnaces, up from the fiery-bellied
Forges, loud, the roar of flame, staccato,
Hammer on hammer, steel on steel, and whirling
Wheels, wheels whirling, grinding, wheels forever
Rushing, rolling, voices, a hundred million
Voices loud in speech, strident, in song too
Strident, voices ribald in song, and mocking

Music that booms, music that blares and gurgles,
Flung on the air and caught again, repeated,
Multiplied, endlessly multiplied by busy
Machines, Oh hammer on hammer and steel on steel,
Wheels and voices and flame, upward this chorus
Ripples and roars, whirling about the slender
Towers, arrogant, proud, lustily tearing
The fragile dawn, shouting aloud in the ardent
Noon, fretfully murmuring still and petulant
When silence and stars timidly claim the night.

IV

Undaunted by the menace of our days,
Untroubled by the temper of our times,
Unflinching in the fever of our ways,
Beauty she brings from old Ionian climes.
Proserpine loved her and she danced with Pan,
The Pythoness has whispered in her ears,
With wonder that once moved the soul of Man
She challenges these gross and barren years.

Ah, can we still the whirling of our wheel
To watch the dawn and dance beside the sea?
Still the staccato hammer of steel on steel
While Orpheus laments Eurydice?
Shall this glad Dryad droop in our torrid noon,
Or shall we have our youth back, strong and fleet,
And dance with her beneath some imminent moon,
Led by the laughter of intrepid feet?

Vale, Vale!

White petals float on the air, and turn, and gleam in the
    sun, but downward; they are still, on the ground.
Crisp leaves scurrying under the moon grow heavy with
    dew; there is an end of gay motion.
The swallow's arced flight is over, the lark wearies of
    heaven, the flute is emptied of sound.
The beautiful winged ship lies broken at the edge of
    ocean.

Oh monstrous!—the hell-black horses come thundering up
    from Dis,
The remorseless arm of the god has snatched her, our
    Proserpine; she is gone.
Never a wing in the blue but is furled at last, and never
    a song but shall cease,
And in the end white feet that dance by the sea pace
    slowly by Acheron.

I saw Pacific's opal waves grow grey, and I heard its
    reproaches spoken,
It cried to the Middle Sea, Where is my Beautiful One?
And the Middle Sea replied, Is not even Niké Apteros
    broken?
Yet is she beautiful and holy, even unto the last day of the
    sun!

MACDOWELL: AN ELEGY

I

His hand indeed no more shall touch the keys,
Caressing or commanding.
At no green portal standing
Henceforth shall he hear
The murmurous birth of woodland harmonies
With mortal ear.
His eyes now close
Forever to the rose,
His voice is still.
Never on the hill
His foot shall press again.
He is done with gladness,
He is done with sadness,
He is done with pain.

Oh mourn him on the mountain
And praise him on the plain.

II

Now let us like that shepherd folk of old
People the heavens with our heroes, changed
To the immortal glory of bright stars.
There is that forest-hero, fabled first
Sower of corn on this broad continent,
And there that constellation of great souls
Who brought the mystic bread and wine, and there
That galaxy of high intrepid hearts
Who wrote the epic of our liberties
And signed it with the sword. How brightly flames
That troubled star whose days the raven shadowed,

Our Israfel, who gave us poetry.
And how serene that luminous sage who lit
In quiet Concord our first lamp of wisdom.
Make place, make place, Immortals, and give ear!
This is the morningstar of our high music,
That waited through the centuries for his touch.

He has taken the tang of pine and spruce and hemlock,
Green sunlight filtering through birch and maple,
Little waters wandering down rocky glens,
And woven them to music. He has taken
The murmurous voices of broad-bosomed rivers,
The rustling voices of horizonless prairies,
The mighty iterant surges of great seas
That shout against our shores, the boisterous winds
That in huge play ruffle our shaggy mountains,
And woven them to music. He remembers
The chant of redskinned huntsmen in the ruddy
Glow of tribal fires, he has noted
The eagle poised, appalling, in the air,
And what of eagle there is in our souls
And what of viking and of voyager,
What heritage the many races brought
Of their long dim traditions—from the fjords,
From the rose-gardens of old England, from
The sunny Irish plains and Highland glens,
And he has woven all of them to music,
Our own at last, our own, American.
Make place for him, Immortals, in our skies!
This song that was he has sung itself to silence,
Silence, the perfect end of every song.

Only as we are saddened when music ceases,

When the entwining harmonies at last
End in a perfect chord, only but so
Mourn we his passing. Death is part of being.
He was, he sang, and he wrought music for us,
And he has gone to join the great of soul
Where the Dear Master, Maker of All Music,
Guides the andante of the singing stars
And the ineffable chorus of seraphim.
There he is part of endless Harmony.
And we have still the beauty of him forever
To measure our souls by. Master, Hail and Farewell!

NORTHWARD

Northward, northward!—the whole world for our own!
This world's an anvil whereupon our will,
Our strength and skill,
Must hammer out a destiny unknown.
And we must fill
With the soul's forges every sullen zone,
Even that one here where Death sits throned in cold upon
    an icy throne.

Forward, forward!
Our life's one law: To grow!
Burdened and broken the sad centuries go,
Scarred with our cruel failures—yet one saw
The Deluge cheated of the just man Noah.
And one was glad to see the Chosen stand
Upon the threshold of the Promised Land.
One saw an Emperor conquered by the Cross.
And where the waters flow
Between the yearning continents, and toss
Their futile waves, one century knew how
Brave Brendan marked a pathway with his prow,
And even so
Columbus led the eager race anew.
One saw the few
Determined pioneers of all the race
Reject an empire's dominance and trace
For Freedom's feet a broad unbounded way.
And that great cycle which was yesterday
More marvels than its banded forbears knew—
Winds and the lightnings doing Man's decree,
And Nature's riddles read that all may see.

Yet more to do
Remains than all that has been done, and we,
We are the doers, the appointed doers we.

Northward!
The fearless Vikings shrunk aghast
From the inscrutable, vast
And terrible portals closing toward the Pole.
Yet by our modern breed grim Cold's control
Is broken more and more, until at last
One Man
Dashes triumphantly to that last goal
Where sits the Eternal Midas whose sad hand
Turns not to gold, but ice, what touches it.
The treacherous floor that is not sea nor land
Sinks under him, the frore floes crash and split,
Weird luminous darkness wavers warnings
Through the long night unlit by mornings,
Deadly distillments of the lethal cold
Subtly into his veins creep unawares,
But he is bold
With courage of great purpose, and he dares
Press northward still, still northward, northward fares—
Till in a moment tremulous with awe,
Silent amid white silence, lo he stands
A victor, at the Pole!
And on his soul
He feels Time's benediction, he who vindicates the Law.
Onward, forever onward!
What though the earth be bounded by the Poles,
Our still insatiate souls
Thirst for the wine of all the worlds, and thirst
For God's own mystic wine; and all the goals

With glory won, we make the sunrise wharves
Whence to new voyage, with aspiring sail,
Freighted with potencies, we start, as first
The savage from his murky vale
Started the heights to scale.
For still abides one Law,
Challenging: Ye shall grow,
Rest not, forward go!
And he who hears and does, he shall know glory, he shall
    be crowned with awe.

HYMN FOR THANKSGIVING DAY

The sickle is dulled of the reaping and the threshing-
floor is bare.
The dust of night's in the air.
The peace of the weary is ours.
All day we have taken the fruit and the grain and the seeds
of the flowers.

The ev'ning is chill.
It is good now to gather in peace by the flames of the fire.
We have done now the deed that we did for our need and
desire,
We have wrought our will.

And now for the boon of abundance and golden increase
And immuréd peace
Shall we thank our God?
Bethink us, amid His indulgence, the might of His rod?

Shall we be as the maple and oak,
To the earth give our gold, offer only bare boughs to the
sky?
Nay, the pine stayeth green while the Winter growls
sullenly by,
And doth not revoke

For soft days or stern days the pledge of its constancy.
Shall we not be
Also the same through all days,
Giving thanks when the battle breaks on us, in toil giving
praise?

O Father who saw at the dawn
That the folly of Pride would be the lush weed of our sin,
There is better than that in our hearts, O enter therein,
A light burneth, though wan

And weak be the flame, yet it gloweth, our Humility.
Ah how can it be
Trimmed o' the wick
And replenished with oil to burn brightly and golden and
    quick?

For deep in our hearts
We wish to be thankful through lean years and fat with-
    out change,
Knowing that here Thou hast set for the spirit a range.
We would play well our parts,

Making America throb with the building of souls and
    with works that are good.
Yea and we would,
And before the last Autumn we will
Build a temple from ocean to ocean where deeds never still

Melodiously shall proclaim
Thanksgiving forever that Thou hast set here to our hand
So wondrous a mystical harvest, that Thou dost demand
Sheaves bound in Thy name,
Yea, supersubstantial sheaves of strong souls that have
    grown
Fain to be known
As the corn of Thine occident field:
O Yielder of All, can America worthily thank Thee till
    such be her yield?

In the mellowing light
Of the goldenest days that precede the grey days of the
    year,
We sing Thee our harvesting song and we pray Thee to
    hear
In the midst of Thy might:

> Toil is given to us,
>   So shall we give thanks.
> Power worketh through us,
> Spending shall renew us,
>   Lord, receive our thanks!
> Not for the garnering,
> But for the mighty thing
> We must do, travailing,—
> For the journey and its length,
> For the task and for our strength,
> For the toil and tears and laughter
> And the peace that cometh after,
> For these, for these O Father,
>   Take Thou, take Thou, our Thanks!

MARY'S BABY

Joseph mild and gentle bent above the straw.
A pale girl, a frail girl suffering he saw.
"O my Love, my Mary, my Bride, I pity thee!"
"Nay, Dear," said Mary, "All is well with me."
"Baby, my Baby, O my Babe," she sang.
Suddenly the silvery night all with music rang.

Angels leading shepherds, shepherds leading sheep:
The silence of worship broke the mother's sleep.
All the meek and lowly of all the world were there.
Smiling she showed them that her Babe was fair.
"Baby, my Baby," kissing Him she said.
Suddenly a flaming star through the heavens sped.

Three old men and weary knelt them side by side,
The world's wealth forswearing, majesty and pride.
Worldly might and wisdom before a Child bent low:
Weeping, Maid Mary said "I love Him so!"
"Baby, my Baby," and the Baby slept.
Far away up Calvary a burdened shadow crept.*

* In an earlier version of this poem (1915), the last line read:
"Suddenly on Calvary all the olives wept."

A NIGHT ON THE HILL

One night, one grey night when clouds hurried across the
stars
And the wind was swift and cold and full of a troubling
cry,
I quenched my lamp and opened my door and dropped
the bars
And went forth into a meadow past seas of shuddering
rye,
And over a field that ghostly lay under a ghostly sky,
And stumblingly I ran that the wind might blow more
swiftly by,
And I fell in weary delight by an old oak clenched with
scars,
And I trembled a-thrill with cold, and was content to lie.
And the glory of God's wild mirth was revealed to me,
And I saw how the elements played at a game through
space
How the wind was mad with a vast impetuous glee,
And a starry gladness broke on the sky's pale face.
White naked runners in the dark, the clouds a-race,
And virginal snowy dancers veiled with lace.
And an ancient laughter roared through the rocking tree,
And ripples of elfin joy sang the flowers of that place.
And I lay like a mossy rock on the side of the hill,
And the spin of the rolling world was a dizzy thing,
And I heard when the winds a moment were suddenly still
The cheery and lusty song that the huge tongues sing,
The tongues of flame leagues deep in earth's hollowing.
Far off I knew the great seas leapt in a ring.
And I rose with joy in my heart and peace on my will
And sought the fire on my hearth and my home's enfolding
wing.

66

KINE OF THE HILLS

Grave kine of the hills,
When I call you at fall of night
It is sunlight that fills
Your udders white.

I drive you East
Toward the unveiling morn.
The silent laughter of the sun
Glints on each burnished horn
And aureoles each beast
And glorifies each one.

All day on the hills,
In the wild meadows,
In the whispering copse,
In the wavering shadows,
But longest in the sunlight—
The yellow wine that spills
In golden waves about you!
And when I come and rout you
And shout you
To the West,
Where the clouds and the hills
Like lips overfain
Twilight's goblet drain
Of its last drops and its best,
It is sunlight—sunlight—sunlight that fills
Each rounded udder,
My kine of the hills!
Your shaggy coats are golden,
Golden and warm.
Your large eyes are languid

Like hours without storm,
Like pools of quiet
Where sunbeams swarm.

Here I draw from you
In the grey dusk,
Sweet as new wine,
Fragrant as musk,
The blood of gold flowers
And yellow grass
You cropped on the hills,
In the crooked pass.
Music to my ears
Fall the streams that fill the pails,
A treasure to mine eyes,
A wealth that never fails.
Oh, life in my veins and a joy my heart that fills
Is the milk of my kine, that was sunlight on the hills.

HUNTINGTON STREET, BROOKLYN

Huntington Street is a little street,
It's far from stylish and scarcely neat,
It starts at a dock and ends in a ditch.
Go from one end, I don't care which,
Right to the other end all the way
And you won't find much that is bright or gay.
Yet the little houses of Huntington Street
Are a pleasant sight for the eyes to meet,
Being old and simple and quaint and strong,
As they long have stood and will stand there long,
Each content in its cozy place
And showing the world a cheerful face.

Now surely it was this sturdy smile
The little old houses wear all the while
That lured the lean trees of Huntington Street
To hurry and hasten the Spring to greet,
With a lyric of leaves spread out in the sun
Ere any tree elsewhere had begun.
Oh, first of all in the city's grey
They started their green dance one fine day,
And there wasn't in all the North so sweet
A spot as dingy Huntington Street,
Looking end to end, and I don't care which,
Where it starts at a dock or ends in a ditch.

THE TENTS OF BOHEMIA

We who are weary,
We who are lost,
Gather at night,
And we are as boats
On a black wave tost
And have no light.

O pitying moon
We have shut you out
With a tent of words,
But I would we were
As a ghostly rout
Or as shadowy herds.

We have turned from the stars
And the wandering clouds
And the color of night,
And we chatter and drink
In the dark that shrouds
The wandering light.

O murmurous fields,
Where the color of night
Moves over dark trees,
And the flood of the moon
To the eyes gives sight,
To the soul gives peace!

IN A CAFÉ

For all the glare of the lights
That seem to leave nothing hidden,
The ancient luminous shadows
Fall here, even here, unbidden.

The music is overloud
And the laughter akin to cries,
But the old significant silences
Sometimes conquer and rise.

See, in these futile revels,
Dimly, an ancient grace—
Bewildered Beauty haunting
Each weary or wanton face.

Here where all folly flaunts
Shameless, for all to see,
I am suddenly aware
Of wisdom and mystery.

ONE SEEN IN BOHEMIA

Brown scarf and red-brown hair and pale small face,
Had my love been with me to-night I had said
"Here is one made for dreams come into this place.
Long ago surely a prince would have crowned that head,
And called upon lords and people to bow to her delicate
    grace,
And called upon lords and bishops to bow where she should
    tread.
Nay but a prince, had he met her under the trees
When he followed the red buck over the brown dry leaves
With the cry of the hounds in his ears, would have for-
    gotten these,
And his stately queen, and honor, and all that grieves,
For a secret hour in her arms and the flame of her red-
    brown hair."
And my Love would have answered, "Aye, she is fair,
Somehow like red-brown fluttering frail small leaves.
Do you not see how the hollow laughter, the music, the
    glare,
And wine and words are warring upon her there?"

WOMEN WITH SHAWLS

By my windows which look out
On a polite and pleasant street,
There often pass
Women of the squalid quarter down the hill :
Creatures of timid faith and querulous doubt,
Brief love and little song and small deceit,
Brief sleep, long toil, a roof, a rag, and meat—
Patience beneath unrealized defeat,
Mortgaged too deep to fate, alas !
To leave much scope for will.
And they are slow and large and ponderous,
And are not beautiful as all women should be,
For under life's incessant mockery
Those things that most make woman beauteous,
Serenity, wonder, gentleness, have quite gone.
Dull as a burdened river they go on,
With no complaint, no choice, no change, no thrill,
Brown clods with so much muscle, so much nerve,
A womb and two breasts each, who still must serve
As fate directs, until
Fate bids them be quite still.
I fancy they are quiet when they go.
And so
They pass, each folded in a sullen shawl,
Death's froward symbol, Life's ironic pall.

FOR MUSIC STIRS OLD THOUGHTS

One day when I was very glad,
　One cloudless afternoon,
I played upon my violin
　An old remembered tune—
Played for the happiness I had,
　The joys I hoped for soon.

An old man sitting in the sun
　Grew rapt to hear me play.
The look that came upon his face
　Meant more than I can say.
And when a mist was in his eyes
　He rose and went away.

A PRAYER OF VERY OLD MEN

Ah, Time, too cruel, your harpy years
Having stolen our laughter, steal our tears.
Oh, being content our mirth to keep,
Relent, relent and let us weep!

A HOPE AT LEAST

Its lines are all unwritten, and afar
In quiet caverns of the morning, wait
The rhythms it must hurl against the Gate,
And in the nebula of an unborn star
Unborn its high predestinate glories are.
But the winged magic that must guide it straight
To quickening hearts, will call me soon or late
From some far wind, some word vernacular.

Oh, there will be rare revelry in my soul,
As when a king's house glows with sudden sound
To hail the newborn man-child of a king,
And where the immortal stars of beauty roll
Through the vast heavens of thought that have no bound,
New flame will leap when my true song I sing.

NO ART CAN TELL

The bright dream burning deep at heart,
No hand has seized, no word has told it.
Melodies that could unfold it
Still elude our subtlest art.
Form we mould in paint and granite,
Doing so our passionate duty,
Fronts the world with wondrous beauty,
But we weep to see and scan it.
That is why we go despairing
In a world of love and laughter,
Heed no past and no hereafter,
Find no rest in all our faring.
That is why we are the sad.
What shall keep our hearts from breaking?
Still unmade for all our making!
Naught to tell the dream we had!

2. Poems, 1924-1932

BAGPIPES

I heard the pipes go by
while the low sun silvered the lake,
And I bade my heart be high
for their sake and for your sake,
Since even in this mean day
wild music flung aloud
mocks at the things men say,
And a passionate and proud
young head holds Time at bay.
Beauty stirs in her shroud.

TO AENGUS GOD OF LOVE
AND HIS COMPANY OF BIRDS

Even the swift god
comes to the weary mile.
Rest the radiant feet,
furl the great wings awhile.
The shy mice of heaven
peep out with shining eyes;
I hear your birds complaining
with querulous faint cries.
Dust dims their crimson,
dew weights their beat:
let them walk in my garden
on frail coral feet.
Bid them hush an hour
their twittering song,
And listen to the music
I hear day-long.

For eager and unresting,
an argent flight of wings,
a dappled bright bevy
circles me and sings,
Sweet sudden fragments,
delirious high strains,
sharp in the marrow,
fiery in the veins,
And all they sing of,
tremulous or clear,
is how my Love is lovely,
and how my Dear is dear,
Precious and perilous,
whimsical and fair,

with moon-kindled eyes
and sun-spun hair,
And lips like berries
cool in the shade,
and apple-breasts
where my head was laid,
And how she yielded
and how she denied,
Beautiful in passion,
beautiful in pride.

I hold out my hands
but they will not alight,
They will not be quiet
day or night—
Oh circle close,
implacable birds,
That I may snare you
in nets of words!

A FRAGMENT

There came a dawn to white Abydos' towers
When Hero, tearless, all her tears being shed,
Knew suddenly the end of those hushed hours
When her strong laughing boy, with wave-drenched head,
Would shake the sea from him, and make the cliff their bed.
Her heart stood still, clutched by the empty years;
But then this thought came flooding like a tide,
Though love is over, yet love was! The spears
Of grief were broken on her remembering pride.

LOVE IS A SEA

Love is a sea that is there, under all life,
always, inexhaustible waters ; it must have fountains,
to find the upper air, to flow, to sing on the mountains,
to fill cool cups for our caked lips, salt with strife.
She is such. She is a fountain, very abundant.
As the sap mounts in the birch-tree, the sweet waters
flow upward through her, sweet among the daughters.
She is a green place among the rocks. Ascendant,
the waters find her and flow through her as a spring.
If she hold out her hands love falls on you ; cooler than
    rain
that fingers the roots of the grasses, caressing and fain.
If she enfold you, the waters are gathering,
a river, a bearer of life, surging, fecundant,
up from the caverns, the deep caves under the mountains
where love is cool waters, upwelling, seeking fountains.
She is such ; a fountain of love, very abundant.

YOUR OTHER LOVERS

Your other lovers? What are they to me?
When has a star been ravished from the skies
By all the rapt millenniums of eyes?
What keel has stolen a splendor from the sea?
Not only I upon a windy hill
Have stood bareheaded calling April fair
When she flings blossoms slanting down the air.
Who shall forbid the brimming cup to spill?

Indeed these fools can never do me wrong,
Who thinking that they know you, never guess
The swift elusive reticent loveliness
You show me, in the silence under the song,
And though they pluck your rose they have my scorn,
For only on my brow you press the thorn.

FOR AUGUSTINE DUNCAN

All work that stands up in the sun,
deep in the soul was first begun.
No cunning play of light and shade
explains how pictured beauty's made.
Light steps that eagerly advance
are not the meaning of the dance.
The poet breaking sensual bars
and looping his lines about the stars,
his tenuous net has first designed
on the taut loom of the mind.
Ah no man hears with outer sense
Eternity's grave eloquence,
nor needs, for Beauty's swift surprise,
the feeble evidence of eyes.

The lamp he sees by cannot falter.
Swung before the spirit's altar,
its passionate creative fire
guides his dauntless high desire.
Sorrow may robe him like the night—
his soul leaps forth, creating light!

REPLYING TO THE MANY KIND FRIENDS
WHO ASK ME IF I NO LONGER
WRITE POETRY

Music is writ by the deaf
and poems by the blind.
The sage who utters wisdom
has little on the mind.
Before I had to use them
to find my way about,
Mine eyes would let in Beauty
and shut Time out.
When I was able
to keep the world hid,
Beauty would nestle
under each lid.
When I heard nothing,
there echoed in my ears
Certain cadenzas
from the Symphony of Spheres.
And in a mind
sinless of thought,
Fragments of wisdom
casually caught.

Now, what would you?
Mind, ears and eyes
must guard me like sentinels
and serve me like spies.
They must be wide open
to see and to hear
All that is obvious
and all that is near,
And to think shrewd thoughts

with logic and reason,
And know what the time is
and what's the season.

So while I must think
and see and hear
And hold my soul taut
to grapple Fear,
The leering tyrant
of the world I live in,
Swift to crush me
if I give in,
Beauty cannot come
stealing from behind,
Nor fragments of wisdom
catch in the mind.
The best I can do
is now and then to fashion
Some measured thought
with guarded passion.
But till I'm blind again
and deaf, I assure you,
I'll write no poems
to lift and allure you.

3. *Antigone*

FOREWORD

This redaction of Sophokles' play having come into being largely by chance, a word of explanation seems called for.

It all began when the Rev. William Norman Guthrie, whose ideas in religion some look at askance, but whose taste in matters artistic none may question, sponsored a reading, at his Church of St. Mark's-in-the-Bouwerie, New York, of the *King Oedipus* as done into prose and lyric verse by William Butler Yeats. This proved so moving that Dr. Guthrie formed a purpose to have the *Antigone* read the next year. Seven weeks before the date set, he discovered that none of the eight or nine versions of the play in his library pleased him. One was Sir Richard Jebb's literal translation—scholarly, awkward, not meant for reading aloud. The others were renditions into blank verse and imitation ode-forms, mostly the exercises of leisurely Church of England clergymen. These were replete with noble lines in the grand manner; but compared with the simplicity achieved by the sure touch of Yeats, they

93

seemed pretentious and trite, as they were clearly less suited to the comprehension of the modern reader or hearer.

Therefore Dr. Guthrie, being a practical man, decided to have a new text prepared to order, in the manner used by the greatest of living poets for his *King Oedipus*—and since then, for his version of the *Oedipus at Colonus*. He called me by telephone one day and asked me to do it, saying he considered me best qualified among American poets for the task. Interpreting this to mean that I was the only versifier he could readily reach at the time, I reminded him that if Shakespeare had little Latin and less Greek, I had less Latin and no Greek; but when it was explained that I was expected to work from Jebb, and in the manner of Yeats, I made terms and undertook the commission. Being a free-lance hack writer at the time, I did the *Antigone* just after completing a book setting forth how the world's greatest life insurance agent wrote sixteen million dollars' worth of business in a year, and just before starting the first draft for a Code for American Industry to be sponsored by a committee of the Taylor Society. My *Antigone* was read at St. Mark's-in-the-Bouwerie on October 19, 1930, by Professor Davis Edwards of the Divinity School, University of Chicago; beautifully and powerfully read; not a few tears were shed in the audience.

Consciousness of certain glaring faults made me revise the text, and then, perhaps unfortunately, it seemed just a bit too good to consign to immediate oblivion.

I have little of critical or scholarly value to offer in observation upon the *Antigone*. It does seem to me that the theory held by some, that Antigone's love for Polyneikes was incestuous, turns out to be merely ingenious in contrast with the simpler understanding of her devotion as not at all greater than the love that may often be observed between members of a family, particularly where they are united by trial and tragedy. If, as Mr. Edmund Wilson alleges, Jebb took liberties with the text in order to make it appear that Antigone was in love with Haemon, it can only be said that Jebb did not make a very good job of it. No work of literature even from classic times bears less trace of romantic love than this play. Clearly, Sophokles brings Haemon into the action solely to add the scene between him and his father to the crescendo of fatal obstinacy which ends in the pitiable stripping of Kreon of his pride and his happiness alike.

The plays of Sophokles are close-knit, and their tragedy strikes like short swift blows, where Euripides thrashes about excitedly. There is merit in both methods. The *Antigone* exhibits one weakness more characteristic of Euripides; it has not one climax, but two. In fact, when the drama of Antigone is finished with that march to the tomb, to the music of the maiden's melodious lament, the drama of Kreon goes on to a separate climax; so that it is his tragedy that moves us at the end, and is celebrated in the last chorus. Dramatically less than perfect though it is, this great symbolic story of conscience confronting law and love defying power is infinitely moving.

Many of the dramas enacted in the theater of Athens, shadowed by the Acropolis, on whose summit the Parthenon reared its proud loveliness against the violet sky, are well-suited to modern understanding; dealing as they do essentially with unchanging human emotions and passions. But until the sure perception of Mr. Yeats found the way to make them live in the interest of the modern reader and beholder, they remained honored but unread, "classics" gathering dust on the shelves. This book is a small contribution to the work of restoring some of the greatest works of all literature to our own living times.

No one knows how Greek actually sounded on the lips of the contemporaries of Perikles. That there was majestic music in, for instance, Sophokles, can be clearly sensed; but English blank verse and English ode-forms have no more relation to that mighty music than plain prose has, and simple lyric verse. And since plain prose and simple verse make clear and living what blank verse and ode-forms keep academic and remote, I am sure that others than I will follow the example of Yeats in resorting to this manner of restoring Athenian tragedy to the body of living literature.

I call my text a redaction and not a version because "version" implies change, and I have taken no liberties with the large outlines of the story; but "redaction" implies merely re-arrangement. I speak of this redaction as done into the American language because it is written in the speech I use every day, and as I was born in America and have never traveled elsewhere, I take it that the language I speak is the American language.

I have in the case of most proper and place names occurring in the text used the spelling which comes nearer the Greek original, instead of the more familiar Latin forms, because I prefer the former. The chief differences are the use of *k* instead of *c* and of *o* instead of *u*, particularly before *s*. However, to avoid diverting attention from the play to scholarly minutiæ, I have let the Latin spelling stand in some firmly established words, as for instance, "Zeus."

SHAEMAS O'SHEEL

THE ARGUMENT

Oedipus reigned as king in Thebes until, in horror at the discovery that he had killed his own father and married his own mother, he put out his eyes and fled. Subsequently, while under the protection of Theseus in the Athenian land, he had been miraculously translated from this world to the world below. These things were set forth by Sophokles in *King Oedipus* and *Oedipus at Koloneos*.

The rule of Thebes passed to the sons of Oedipus, Eteokles and Polyneikes, who were to govern individually in alternate years; and their uncle Kreon was associated with them in the sovereignty. But at the end of a year Eteokles refused to render the sway to Polyneikes, who, driven from the city, went among the Argives, his wife's people, and raised an army which he led against Thebes. The invaders were defeated before the seven gates of the city; and Eteokles and Polyneikes fell by each other's hand. Kreon, by this event, came to the sole rule of the land of Kadmos; and, indignant that Polyneikes had warred upon his native city, ordered that his corpse (and those, too, of the fallen Argives, as appears by implication in the first speeches of Antigone and Ismene, and clearly later in the action) should be left without burial rites.

In the belief of the Greeks, if a corpse were left unburied, or if, at least, it were not honored by such funeral rites as the sprinkling of earth and the pouring of libations over it, the soul could not enter Hades, the Nether World of souls, the abode of the Gods below. Therefore to refuse burial rites to the dead was a violation of the laws of Zeus, the depth of sacrilege, a reprisal past all justice, no matter how great had been the crime of the departed. For the kin of one dead to fail in the duty of giving burial or paying ritual honor to the corpse, was the deepest of sins.

Thus things stand when the action is begun by Antigone and Ismene, daughters of Oedipus, sisters of Eteokles and Polyneikes, kinswomen of Kreon.

The scene is an open space before the house of Kreon. The house is at the back, with gates opening from it. On the right, the city is to be supposed; to the left and in the distance, the Theban plain and the hills rising beyond it.

THE PLAY

[*Antigone and Ismene come
from the King's house.*]

ANTIGONE: Ismene, O my dear, my little sister, of all
the griefs bequeathed us by our father Oedipus, is there
any that Zeus will spare us while we live? There is no sor-
row and no shame we have not known. And now what is
this new edict they tell about, that our Captain has pub-
lished all through Thebes? Do you know? Have you
heard? Or is it kept from you that our friends are threat-
ened with the punishment due to foes?

ISMENE: I have heard no news, Antigone, glad or sad,
about our friends, since we two sisters lost two brothers
at a single blow; and since the Argive army fled last night,
I do not know whether my fortune is better or worse.

ANTIGONE: I know, I know it well. That is why I sent
for you to come outside the gates, to speak to you alone.

ISMENE: What is it? I can see that you are troubled.

ANTIGONE: Should I not be?—when Kreon gives

99

honors to one of our brothers, but condemns the other to shame? Eteokles, they say, he has laid in the earth with due observance of right and custom, that all may be well with him among the shades below. But the poor corpse of Polyneikes—it has been published to the city that none shall bury him, none shall mourn him; but he shall be left unwept and unsepulchred, and the birds are welcome to feast upon him!

Such, they say, are the orders the good Kreon has given for you and me—yes, for me! He is coming now to make his wishes clear; and it is no light matter, for whoever disobeys him is condemned to death by stoning before all the people. Now you know!—and now you will show whether you are nobly bred, or the unworthy daughter of a noble line.

ISMENE: Sister, sister!—if we are caught in this web, what could I do to loose or tighten the knot?

ANTIGONE: Decide if you will share the work and the danger.

ISMENE: What are you planning?—what are you thinking of?

ANTIGONE: Will you help this hand to lift the dead?

ISMENE: Oh, you would bury him!—when it is forbidden to anyone in Thebes?

ANTIGONE: He is still my brother, if he is not yours. No one shall say I failed in my duty to him.

ISMENE: But how can you dare, when Kreon has forbidden it?

ANTIGONE: He has no right to keep me from my own.

ISMENE: Alas, sister, remember how our father perished, hated and scorned, when he had struck out his eyes in horror of the sins his own persistency had brought to

100

light. Remember how she who was both his mother and his wife hung herself with a twisted cord. And only yesterday our two brothers came to their terrible end, each by the other's hand. Now only we two are left, and we are all alone. Think how we shall perish, more miserably than all the rest, if in defiance of the law we brave the King's decree and the King's power. No, no, we must remember we were born women, not meant to strive with men. We are in the grip of those stronger than ourselves, and must obey them in this and in things still more cruel. Therefore I will ask forgiveness of the gods and spirits who dwell below, for they will see that I yield to force, and I will hearken to our rulers. It is foolish to be too zealous even in a good cause.

ANTIGONE: I will not urge you. No, if you wished to join me now I would not let you. Do as you think best. As for me, I will bury him; and if I die for that, I am content. I shall rest like a loved one with him whom I have loved, innocent in my guilt. For I owe a longer allegiance to the dead than to the living; I must dwell with them forever. You, if you wish, may dishonor the laws which the gods have established.

ISMENE: I would not dishonor them, but to defy the State—I am not strong enough for that!

ANTIGONE: Well, make your excuses—I am going now to heap the earth above the brother whom I love.

ISMENE: Oh, I fear something terrible will happen to you!

ANTIGONE: Fear not for me; but look to your own fate.

ISMENE: At least, then, tell no one what you intend, but hide it closely—and so too will I.

ANTIGONE: No, but cry it aloud! I will condemn you

101

more if you are silent than if you proclaim my deed to all.

ISMENE: You have so hot a heart for deeds that make the blood run cold!

ANTIGONE: My deeds will please those they are meant to please.

ISMENE: Ah yes, if you can do what you plan—but you cannot.

ANTIGONE: When my strength fails, I shall confess my failure.

ISMENE: The impossible should not be tried at all.

ANTIGONE: If you say such things I will hate you, and the dead will haunt you!—But leave me, and the folly that is mine alone, to suffer what I must; for I shall not suffer anything so dreadful as an ignoble death.

ISMENE: Go then, if you must, though your errand is mad; and be sure of this, my love goes with you!

[*Antigone goes toward the plain. Ismene retires into the King's house. The Chorus, being the elders of Thebes, comes into the place before the house.*]

CHORUS:

Over the waters, see!—over the stream of Dirke, the golden eye of the dawn opens on the seven gates;
Terror crouched in the night, how welcome to Thebes is the morning, when the warriors of the white shields flee from the spears of the sun.

From Argos mailed they came, swords drawn for Polyneikes; like eagles that scream in the air these plumed ones fell on our land.
They ravened around our towers, and burst the doors of

102

our dwellings; their spears sniffed at our blood—but they fled without quenching that thirst.

They heaped the eager pine-boughs, flaming, against our bastions, calling upon Hephaestos; but he the fire-god failed them.
The clash of battle was loud, the clamor beloved of the war-god; but a thing they found too hard was to conquer the dragon's brood.

And a thing abhorred by Zeus is the boastful tongue of the haughty: one proud chief, armored in gold, with triumph in his throat,
The stormy wave of the foe flung to the crest of our rampart—the god, with a crooked bolt, smites him crashing to earth.

At the seven gates of the city, seven of the host's grim captains yielded to Zeus who turns the tide of battle, their arms of bronze;
And woe to those two sons of the same father and mother, they crossed their angry spears, and brought each other low.

But now since Victory, most desired of all men, to Thebes of the many chariots has come scattering joy,
Let us forget the wars, and dance before the temples; and Bacchos be our leader, loved by the land of Thebes!

But see, the King of this land comes yonder—Kreon, son of Menoekeos, our new ruler by virtue of the new turn the gods have given things. What counsel is he pondering, that he has called by special summons this gathering of the elders?

KREON: Sirs, our State has been like a ship tossed by stormy waves; but thanks to the gods, it sails once more upon a steady keel. You I have summoned here apart from all the people because I remember that of old you had great reverence for the royal power of Laius; and I know how you upheld Oedipus when he ruled this land, and, when he died, you loyally supported his two sons. Those sons have fallen, both in one moment, each smitten by the other, each stained with a brother's blood; now I possess the throne and all its powers, since I am nearest kindred of the dead.

No man's worthiness to rule can be known until his mind and soul have been tested by the duties of government and law-giving. For my part, I have always held that any man who is the supreme guardian of the State, and who fails in his duty through fear, remaining silent when evil is done, is base and contemptible; nor have I any regard for him who puts friendship above the common welfare. Zeus, who sees all things, be my witness that I will not be silent when danger threatens the people; nor will I ever call my country's foe my friend. For our country is the ship that bears us all, and he only is our friend who helps us sail a prosperous course.

Such are the rules by which I will guard this city's greatness; and in keeping with them is the edict I have published touching the sons of Oedipus. For Eteokles, who fell like a true soldier defending his native land, there shall be such funeral as we give the noblest dead. But as to his brother Polyneikes—he who came out of exile and sought to destroy with fire the city of his fathers and the shrines of his fathers' gods—he who thirsted for the blood of his

kin, and would have led into slavery all who escaped death
—as to this man, it has been proclaimed that none shall
honor him, none shall lament over him, but he shall lie un-
buried, a corpse mangled by birds and dogs, a gruesome
thing to see. Such is my way with traitors.

CHORUS: Such is your way, Kreon, son of Menoekeos,
with the false and with the faithful; and you have power,
I know, to give such orders as you please, both for the
dead and for all of us who live.

KREON: Then look to it that my mandate is observed.

CHORUS: Call on some younger man for this hard
task.

KREON: No, watchers of the corpse have been ap-
pointed.

CHORUS: What is this duty, then, you lay on us?

KREON: To side with no one breaking this command.

CHORUS: No man is foolish enough to go courting
death.

KREON: That indeed shall be the penalty; but men
have been lured even to death by the hope of gain.

[*A Guard, coming from the direction
of the plain, approaches Kreon.*]

GUARD: Sire, I will not say that I am out of breath
from hurrying, nor that I have come here on the run; for
in fact my thoughts made me pause more than once, and
even turn in my path, to go back. My mind was telling me
two different things. "Fool," it said to me, "why do you
go where you are sure to be condemned?" And then on the
other hand, "Wretch, tarrying again? If Kreon hears of
this from another, you'll smart for it." Torn between these
fears, I came on slowly and unwillingly, making a short
road long. But at last I got up courage to come to you,

105

and though there is little to my story, I will tell it; for I have got a good grip on one thought—that I can suffer nothing but what is my fate.

KREON: Well, and what is it that makes you so upset?

GUARD: First let me tell you that I did not do the deed and I did not see it done, so it would not be just to make me suffer for it.

KREON: You have a good care for your own skin, and armor yourself well against blame. I take it that you have news to tell?

GUARD: Yes, that I have, but bad news is nothing to be in a hurry about.

KREON: Tell it, man, will you?—tell it and be off.

GUARD: Well, this is it. The corpse—someone has done it funeral honors—sprinkled dust upon it, and other pious rites.

KREON: What—what do you say? What man has dared this deed?

GUARD: That I cannot tell you. There was no sign of a pick being used, no earth torn up the way it is by a mattock. The ground was hard and dry; there was no track of wheels. Whoever did it left no trace; when the first day-watchman showed it to us, we were struck dumb. You couldn't see the dead man at all; not that he was in any grave, but dry dust was strewn that thick all over him. It was the hand of someone warding off a curse did that. There was no sign that any dog or wild beast had been at the body.

Then there were loud words, and hard words, among us of the guard, everyone accusing someone else, 'til we nearly came to blows, and it's a wonder we didn't. Everyone was accused and no one was convicted, and each man stuck to it that he knew nothing about it. We were ready to take red-hot iron in our hands—to walk through fire—to swear by the gods that we did not do the deed and were not in the secret of whoever did it.

At last, when all our disputing got us nowhere, one of the men spoke up in a way that made us look down at the ground in silence and fear; for we could not see how to gainsay him, nor how to escape trouble if we heeded him. What he said was, that this must be reported to you, it was no use hiding it. There was no doubt of it he was right; so we cast lots, and it was my bad luck to win the prize. Here I am, then, as unwelcome as unwilling, I know; for no man likes the bearer of bad news.

CHORUS: O King, my thoughts have been whispering, could this deed perhaps have been the work of gods?

KREON: Silence, before your words fill me with anger, and you prove yourself as foolish as you are old! You say what is not to be borne, that the gods would concern themselves with this corpse. What!—did they cover his nakedness to reward the reverence he paid them, coming to burn their pillared shrines and sacred treasures, to harry their land, to put scorn upon their laws? Do you think it is the way of the gods to honor the wicked? No! From the first there were some in this city who muttered against me, chafing at this edict, wagging their heads in secret; they would not bow to the yoke, not they, like men contented with my rule.

I know well enough, it is such malcontents who have bribed and beguiled these guards to do this deed or let it be done. Nothing so evil as money ever arose among men. It lays cities low, drives peoples from their homes, warps honest souls 'til they give themselves to works of shame; it teaches men to practise villainies and grow familiar with impious deeds.

But the men who did this thing for hire, sooner or later they shall pay the price. Now, as Zeus still has my reverence, know this—I tell you on my oath: Unless you find the very man whose hand strewed dust upon that body, and bring him here before mine eyes, death alone shall not be enough for you, but you shall first be hung up alive until you reveal the truth about this outrage; that henceforth you may have a better idea about how to get money, and learn that it is not wise to grasp at it from any source. I will teach you that ill-gotten gains bring more men to ruin than to prosperity.

GUARD: May I speak? Or shall I turn and go?

KREON: Can you not see that your voice offends me?

GUARD: Are your ears troubled, or your soul?

KREON: And why should you try to fix the seat of my pain?

GUARD: The doer of the deed inflames your mind, but I, only your ears.

KREON: Bah, you are a babbler born!

GUARD: I may be that, but I never did this deed.

KREON: You did, for silver; but you shall pay with your life.

GUARD: It is bad when a judge misjudges.

KREON: Prate about "judgment" all you like; but unless you show me the culprit in this crime, you will admit before long that guilty wages were better never earned.

[*Kreon goes into his house.*]

GUARD: Well, may the guilty man be found, that's all I ask. But whether he's found or not—fate will decide that —you will not see me here again. I have escaped better than I ever hoped or thought—I owe the gods much thanks.

108

[The Guard departs, going toward the plain.]

CHORUS:

Wonders are many in the world, and the wonder of all is
    man.
    With his bit in the teeth of the storm and his faith in a
        fragile prow,
Far he sails, where the waves leap white-fanged, wroth at
    his plan.
    And he has his will of the earth by the strength of his
        hand on the plough.

The birds, the clan of the light heart, he snares with his
    woven cord,
    And the beasts with wary eyes, and the stealthy fish in
        the sea;
That shaggy freedom-lover, the horse, obeys his word,
    And the sullen bull must serve him, for cunning of wit is
        he.

Against all ills providing, he tempers the dark and the
    light,
    The creeping siege of the frost and the arrows of sleet
      · and rain,
The grievous wounds of the daytime and the fever that
    steals in the night;
    Only against Death man arms himself in vain.

With speech and wind-swift thought he builds the State
    to his mood,
    Prospering while he honors the gods and the laws of the
        land.

Yet in his rashness often he scorns the ways that are
good—

May such as walk with evil be far from my hearth and
hand!

[*The Guard re-appears, leading Antigone.*]

CHORUS: But what is this?—what portent from the
gods is this? I am bewildered, for surely this maiden is
Antigone; I know her well.

O luckless daughter of a luckless father, child of
Oedipus, what does this mean? Why have they made you
prisoner? Surely they did not take you in the folly of
breaking the King's laws?

GUARD: Here she is, the doer of the deed! We caught
this girl burying him. But where is Kreon?

CHORUS: Look, he is coming from the house now.

[*Kreon comes from the house.*]

KREON: What is it? What has happened that makes
my coming timely?

GUARD: Sire, a man should never say positively "I will
do this" or "I won't do that," for things happen to change
the mind. I vowed I would not soon come here again, after
the way you scared me, lashing me with your threats. But
there's nothing so pleasant as a happy turn when we've
given up hope, so I have broken my sworn oath to hurry
back here with this girl, who was taken showing grace to
the dead. This time there was no casting of lots; no, this is
my good luck, no one else's. And now, Sire, take her your-
self, question her, examine her, all you please; but I have
a right to free and final quittance of this trouble.

KREON: Stay!—this prisoner—how and where did you
take her?

110

GUARD: She was burying the man; that's all there is to tell you.

KREON: Do you mean what you say? Are you telling the truth?

GUARD: I saw her burying the corpse that you had forbidden to bury. Is that plain and clear?

KREON: What did you see? Did you take her in the act?

GUARD: It happened this way. When we came to the place where he lay, worrying over your threats, we swept away all the dirt, leaving the rotting corpse bare. Then we sat us down on the brow of the hill to windward, so that the smell from him would not strike us. We kept wide awake frightening each other with what you would do to us if we didn't carry out your command. So it went until the sun was bright in the top of the sky, and the heat began to burn. Then suddenly a whirlwind came roaring down, making the sky all black, hiding the plain under clouds of choking dust and leaves torn from the trees. We closed our eyes and bore this plague from the gods.

And when, after a long while, the storm had passed, we saw this girl, and she crying aloud with the sharp cry of a bird in its grief; the way a bird will cry when it sees the nest bare and the nestlings gone, it was that way she lifted up her voice when she saw the corpse uncovered; and she called down dreadful curses on those that did it. Then straightway she scooped up dust in her hands, and she had a shapely ewer of bronze, and she held that high while she honored the dead with three drink-offerings.

We rushed forward at this and closed on our quarry, who was not at all frightened at us. Then we charged her with the past and present offences, and she denied nothing —I was both happy and sorry for that. It is good to

111

escape danger one's self, but hard to bring trouble to one's friends. However, nothing counts with me so much as my own safety.

KREON: You, then—you whose face is bent to the earth—do you confess or do you deny the deed?

ANTIGONE: I did it; I make no denial.

KREON (*to Guard*): You may go your way, wherever you will, free and clear of a grave charge.

(*To Antigone*): Now tell me—not in many words, but briefly—did you know of the edict that forbade what you did?

ANTIGONE: I knew it. How could I help knowing?— it was public.

KREON: And you had the boldness to transgress that law?

ANTIGONE: Yes, for it was not Zeus made such a law; such is not the Justice of the gods. Nor did I think that your decrees had so much force, that a mortal could override the unwritten and unchanging statutes of heaven. For their authority is not of today nor yesterday, but from all time, and no man knows when they were first put forth.

Not through dread of any human power could I answer to the gods for breaking these. That I must die I knew without your edict. But if I am to die before my time, I count that a gain; for who, living as I do in the midst of many woes, would not call death a friend?

It saddens me little, therefore, to come to my end. If I had let my mother's son lie in death an unburied corpse, that would have saddened me, but for myself I do not grieve. And if my acts are foolish in your eyes, it may be that a foolish judge condemns my folly.

CHORUS: The maiden shows herself the passionate

112

daughter of a passionate father, she does not know how to bend the neck.

KREON: Let me remind you that those who are too stiff and stubborn are most often humbled; it is the iron baked too hard in the furnace you will oftenest see snapped and splintered. But I have seen horses that show temper brought to order by a little curb. Too much pride is out of place in one who lives subject to another. This girl was already versed in insolence when she transgressed the law that had been published; and now, behold, a second insult—to boast about it, to exult in her misdeed!

But I am no man, she is the man, if she can carry this off unpunished. No! She is my sister's child, but if she were nearer to me in blood than any who worships Zeus at the altar of my house, she should not escape a dreadful doom —nor her sister either, for indeed I charge her too with plotting this burial.

And summon that sister—for I saw her just now within, raving and out of her wits. That is the way minds plotting evil in the dark give away their secret and convict themselves even before they are found out. But the most intolerable thing is that one who has been caught in wickedness should glory in the crime.

ANTIGONE: Would you do more than slay me?

KREON: No more than that—no, and nothing less.

ANTIGONE: Then why do you delay? Your speeches give me no pleasure, and never will; and my words, I suppose, buzz hatefully in your ear. I am ready; for there is no better way I could prepare for death than by giving burial to my brother. Everyone would say so if their lips were not sealed by fear. But a king has many advantages, he can do and say what he pleases.

KREON: You slander the race of Kadmos; not one of them shares your view of this deed.

ANTIGONE: They see it as I do, but their tails are between their legs.

KREON: They are loyal to their king; are you not ashamed to be otherwise?

ANTIGONE: No; there is nothing shameful in piety to a brother.

KREON: Was it not a brother also who died in the good cause?

ANTIGONE: Born of the same mother and sired by the same father.

KREON: Why then do you dishonor him by honoring that other?

ANTIGONE: The dead will not look upon it that way.

KREON: Yes, if you honor the wicked equally with the virtuous.

ANTIGONE: It was his brother, not his slave, that died.

KREON: One perished ravaging his fatherland, the other defending it.

ANTIGONE: Nevertheless, Hades desires these rites.

KREON: Surely the good are not pleased to be made equal with the evil!

ANTIGONE: Who knows how the gods see good and evil?

KREON: A foe is never a friend—even in death.

ANTIGONE: It is not my nature to join in hating, but in loving.

KREON: Your place, then, is with the dead. If you must love, love them. While I live, no woman shall overbear me.

114

CHORUS: See, Ismene comes through the gate, shedding such tears as loving sisters weep. It seems as if a cloud gathers about her brow and breaks in rain upon her cheek.

KREON: And you, who lurked like a viper in my house, sucking the blood of my honor, while I knew not that I was nursing two reptiles ready to strike at my throne—come, tell me now, will you confess your part in this guilty burial, or will you swear you knew nothing of it?

ISMENE: I am guilty if she is, and share the blame.

ANTIGONE: No, no! Justice will not permit this. You did not consent to the deed, nor would I let you have part in it.

ISMENE: But now that danger threatens you, I am not ashamed to come to your side.

ANTIGONE: Who did the deed, the gods and the dead know; a friend in words is not the friend I love.

ISMENE: Sister, do not reject me, but let me die with you, and duly honor the dead.

ANTIGONE: Do not court death, nor claim a deed to which you did not put your hand. My death will suffice.

ISMENE: How could life be dear to me without you?

ANTIGONE: Ask Kreon, you think highly of his word.

ISMENE: Why taunt me so, when it does you no good?

ANTIGONE: Ah, if I mock you, it is with pain I do it.

ISMENE: Oh tell me, how can I serve you, even now?

ANTIGONE: Save yourself; I do not grudge your escape.

ISMENE: Oh, my grief! Can I not share your fate?

115

ANTIGONE: You chose to live, and I to die.

ISMENE: At least I begged you not to make that choice.

ANTIGONE: This world approved your caution, but the gods my courage.

ISMENE: But now I approve, and so I am guilty too.

ANTIGONE: Ah little sister, be of good cheer, and live. My life has long been given to death, that I might serve the dead.

KREON: Behold, one of these girls turns to folly now, as the other one has ever since she was born.

ISMENE: Yes, Sire, such reason as nature gives us may break under misfortune, and go astray.

KREON: Yours did, when you chose to share evil deeds with the evil.

ISMENE: But I cannot live without her.

KREON: You mistake; she lives no more.

ISMENE: Surely you will not slay your own son's betrothed?

KREON: He can plough other fields.

ISMENE: But he cannot find such love again.

KREON: I will not have an evil wife for my son.

ANTIGONE: Ah, Haemon, my beloved! Dishonored by your father!

KREON: Enough! I'll hear no more of you and your marriage!

CHORUS: Will you indeed rob your son of his bride?

KREON: Death will do that for me.

CHORUS: It seems determined then, that she shall die.

KREON: Determined, yes—for me and for you. No more delay—servants, take them within. Let them know that they are women, not meant to roam abroad. For

116

even the boldest seek to fly when they see Death stretching
his hand their way.

[*Attendants lead Antigone and Ismene
into the house.*]

CHORUS:

Blest are they whose days have not tasted of sorrow:
For if a house has dared the anger of heaven,
Evil strikes at it down the generations,
Wave after wave, like seas that batter a headland.

I see how fate has harried the seed of Labdakos;
Son cannot fly the curse that was laid on the sire,
The doom incurred by the dead must fall on the living:
When gods pursue, no race can find deliverance.

And even these, the last of the children of Oedipus—
Because of the frenzy that rose in a passionate heart,
Because of a handful of blood-stained dust that was
    sprinkled—
The last of the roots is cut, and the light extinguished.

O Zeus, how vain is the mortal will that opposes
The Will Immortal that neither sleeps nor ages,
The Imperturbable Power that on Olympos
Dwells in unclouded glory, the All-Beholding!

Wise was he who said that ancient saying:
Whom the gods bewilder, at last takes evil for virtue;
And let no man lament if his lot is humble—
No great things come to mortals without a curse.

But look, Sire: Haemon, the last of your sons, approaches. I wonder if he comes grieving over the doom of his promised bride, Antigone, and bitter that his marriage-hopes are baffled?

[Haemon comes before his father.]

KREON: We shall know soon, better than seers could tell us. My son, you have heard the irrevocable doom decreed for your betrothed. Do you come to rage against your father, or do you remember the duty of filial love, no matter what I do?

HAEMON: Father, I am yours; and knowing you are wise, I follow the paths you trace for me. No marriage could be more to me than your good guidance.

KREON: Yes, my son, this should be your heart's first law, in all things to obey your father's will. Men pray for dutiful children growing up about them in their homes, that such may pay their father's foe with evil, and honor as their father does, his friend. But if a man begets undutiful children, what shall we say that he has sown, only sorrow for himself and triumph for his enemies? Do not then, my son, thinking of pleasures, put aside reason for a woman's sake. If you brought an evil woman to your bed and home, you would find that such embraces soon grow hateful; and nothing can wound so deeply as to find a loved one false. No, but with loathing, and as if she were your enemy, let this girl go to find a husband in the house of Hades. For she alone in all the city defied and disobeyed me; I have taken her in the act, and I will not be a liar to my people—I will slay her.

Let her appeal all she pleases to the claims of kindred blood. If I am to rear my own kin to evil deeds, certainly I must expect evil among the people. Only a man who rules
118

his own household justly can do justice in the State. If anyone transgresses, and does violence to the laws, or thinks to dictate to the ruler, I will not tolerate it. No!— whoever the city shall appoint to rule, that man must be obeyed, in little things and great things, in just things and unjust; for the man who is a good subject is the one who would be a good ruler, and it is he who in time of war will stand his ground where he is placed, loyal to his comrades and without fear, though the spears fall around him like rain in a storm.

But disobedience is the worst of evils. It desolates households; it ruins cities; it throws the ranks of allies into confusion and rout. On the other hand, note those whose lives are prosperous: they owe it, you will generally find, to obedience. Therefore we must uphold the cause of order; and certainly we must not let a woman defy us. It would be better to fall from power by a man's hand, than to be called weaker than a woman.

CHORUS: Unless the years have stolen our wits, all that you say seems wise.

HAEMON: Father, the gods implant reason in men, the highest of all things that we call our own. I have no skill to prove, and I would not wish to show, that you speak unwisely; and yet another man, too, might have some useful thought. I count it a duty to keep my ears alert for what men say about you, noting especially when they find fault. The people dare not say to your face what would displease you; but I can hear the things murmured in the dark, and the whole city weeps for this maiden. "No woman ever," they say, "so little merited a cruel fate. None was ever doomed to a shameful death for deeds so noble as hers; who, when her brother lay dead from bloody wounds, would not leave him unburied for the birds

119

and the dogs to mangle. Does not so pious an act deserve golden praise?"

Such is the way the people speak in secret. To me, father, nothing is so precious as your welfare. What is there father or son can so rejoice in as the other's fair repute? I pray you therefore do not wear one mood too stubbornly, as if no one else could possibly be right. For the man who thinks he is the only wise man always proves hollow when we sound him. No, though a man be wise, it is no shame for him to learn many things, and to yield at the right time. When the streams rage and overflow in Winter, you know how those trees that yield come safely through the flood; but the stubborn are torn up and perish, root and branch. Consider too, the sailor who keeps his sheet always taut, and never slackens it; presently his boat overturns and his keel floats uppermost.

So, though you are angry, permit reason to move you. If I, young as I am, may offer a thought, I would say it were best if men were by nature always wise; but that being seldom so, it is prudent to listen to those who offer honest counsel.

CHORUS: Sire, it is fitting that you should weigh his words, if he speaks in season; and you, Haemon, should mark your father's words; for on both parts there has been wise speech.

KREON: What! Shall men of our age be schooled by youths like this?

HAEMON: In nothing that does not go with reason; but as to my youth, you should weigh my merits, not my years.

KREON: Is it your merit that you honor the lawless?

HAEMON: I could wish no one to respect evil-doers.

120

KREON: This girl—is she not tainted with that plague?

HAEMON: Our Theban folk deny it, with one voice.

KREON: Shall Thebes, then, tell me how to rule?

HAEMON: Now who speaks like a boy?

KREON: Tell me—am I to rule by my own judgment or the views of others?

HAEMON: That is no city which belongs to one man.

KREON: Is not the city held to be the ruler's?

HAEMON: That kind of monarchy would do well in a desert.

KREON: Ho, this boy, it seems, is the woman's champion!

HAEMON: Yes, if you are a woman, for my concern is for you.

KREON: Shameless, to bandy arguments with your father!

HAEMON: Only because I see you flouting justice.

KREON: Is it wrong for me to respect my royal position?

HAEMON: It is a poor way to respect it, trampling on the laws of the gods.

KREON: This is depravity, putting a woman foremost!

HAEMON: At least you will not find me so depraved that I fear to plead for justice.

KREON: Every word you speak is a plea for that girl.

HAEMON: And for you, and for me, and for the gods below.

KREON: Marry her you shall not, this side the grave.

HAEMON: She must die then, and in dying destroy others?

KREON: Ha, you go so far as open threats?

HAEMON: I speak no threats, but grieve for your fatal stubbornness.

KREON: You shall rue your unwise teaching of wisdom.

HAEMON: If you were not my father, I would call you unwise.

KREON: Slave of a woman, do not think you can cajole me.

HAEMON: Then no one but yourself may speak, you will hear no reason?

KREON: Enough of this—now, by Olympos, you shall smart for baiting me this way! Bring her here, that hateful rebel, that she may die forthwith before his eyes—yes, at her bridegroom's side!

HAEMON: No, no, never think it, I shall not witness her death; but my face your eyes shall never see again. Give your passion its way before those who can endure you!

[*Haemon rushes away.*]

CHORUS: He has gone, O King, in angry haste; a youthful mind, when stung, is impetuous.

KREON: Let him do what he will, let him dream himself more than a common man, but he shall not save those girls from their doom.

CHORUS: Are you indeed determined to slay them both?

KREON: Not the one whose hands are clean of the crime—you do well to remind me of that.

CHORUS: But how will you put the other one to death?

KREON: I will take her where the path is loneliest, and hide her, living, in a rocky vault, with only so much food as the pious laws require, that the city may avoid reproach. There she can pray to Hades, whose gods alone

122

she worships; perhaps they will bargain with death for
her escape. And if they do not, she will learn, too late, that
it is lost labor to revere the dead.

[*Kreon leaves.*]

CHORUS:

Great is love, and what shall prevail against it,
When from the deep and quiet eyes of a maiden
Sallying forth, it mocks at our laws and powers,
Pride and possessions?

Wave of the sea is love, wind on the mountains:
Neither deathless gods nor mortals escape it.
The good it turns to evil, the wise to folly,
All men to madness.

And if a son is angered against his father,
Blame him not, but see who has wrought this frenzy—
She the goddess loveliest and most willful,
Fierce Aphrodite!

[*Antigone is led from the
King's house.*]

But Oh, this is a sight that shakes even my loyalty to
the laws! I cannot stay my tears, when I see Antigone
thus pass on her way to that bridal chamber where we
shall all come at last.

ANTIGONE: See me, citizens of my fatherland, setting
forth on my last journey, looking my last on the sunlight
—soon for me it will be no more; but Death, who hides
us all from the sun, is hasty with me; soon I shall stand
on Acheron's shore, I who have no portion in the song
they sing for brides, nor the evening song before the bridal

chamber; but the Lord of the Dark Lake will be my bridegroom.

CHORUS:

Yet I would give it praise, the way of your going:
Neither did sickness waste nor violence smite you.
Mastering fate in this wise never has mortal
Gone down to Hades.

ANTIGONE: I have heard how in other days a terrible fate befell Niobe, daughter of Tantalos, and how on Mount Sipylos the rock grew around her as ivy grows on a wall. And they say that there on that desolate height, where rain and snow never cease, her tears also never cease to flow beneath her stony lids. I think my doom is like hers.

CHORUS:

She was a goddess, Niobe, born of immortals;
If one of the race of men that is born to perish
Fares like her whose sire had Zeus for father,
Great is the honor.

ANTIGONE: Oh, must you mock me? My city, my city, and you her fortunate sons, in the name of our father's gods can you not wait 'til I am gone—must you taunt me to my face? Ah, river of Dirke, and sacred groves of Thebes, bear witness how no friend weeps for me as I near that rocky chamber, my prison and my tomb!— none weeps for me unhappy, who have no friend in the sun nor in the shadows, no home with the living or the dead.

124

CHORUS:

All too rash was your deed, unhappy maiden,
Boldly daring even the throne of justice:
There you fell. Alas, you must pay to the utmost,
Doom of your father.

ANTIGONE: You touch the quick of all my grief, my bitterest thought—my father's sin and punishment, and how the implacable Fates still harry the famous house of Labdakos. Alas for the horrors of that bed where a mother slept with her son—such parents gave me my miserable being, and now I go to them, accursed, unwed, to share their shadowy home. Alas my brother who married the Argive woman, your death has undone my life!

CHORUS:

Reverence moved your hand, the deed I reverence,
Yet if a man have power over a city,
Scorn of that power he may not bear. O self-willed,
Your rashness slays you!

ANTIGONE: Then it is certain I must take this journey, for none befriends me. There will be no marriage-song; I may not longer even look on the sun. No one mourns my passing, none even weeps.

[Kreon returns.]

KREON: Do you not know that if pleas and lamentations could save the doomed, they would never cease? Away with her, away! And when you have shut her in the vaulted tomb according to my word, leave her, leave her there alone. Let her choose whether she wishes to die, or to live

125

buried in such a home. Our hands are clean as touching this maiden. Only this much is certain—she shall dwell no more in the light.

ANTIGONE: Tomb, my bridal-chamber, eternal prison in the caverned rock, when I come to you I shall find mine own, those many who have perished, who have seen Persephone. Last of all I take that way, and far most miserably of all, my days so few! But I cherish good hope that my coming will be welcome to my father, and pleasant to my mother, and to you, my brother, pleasing too; for each of you in death I washed with my own hands, and dressed for your graves; and I poured drink-offerings over you.

And you too, Polyneikes; for you also in death I tended, and for that I win such recompense as this. Yet the just will say I did rightly in paying you these honors, for it was thus I saw the higher law; but Kreon calls me guilty, brother, and leads me captive on the way to death. No bridal bed, no bridal song have been mine, no joy of marriage, no children at my breast; but thus forlorn and friendless I go living to the grave.

Yet what law of heaven did I offend? Ah, why should I look to the gods any more, for I see they do not hear me, but let me suffer the punishment of the impious for doing a pious deed. If my fate indeed is pleasing to the gods, when I have suffered my doom no doubt I shall learn my sin; but if the sin is with my judges, I wish them no measure of evil greater than they have measured out to me.

CHORUS: Still the same tempest vexes this maiden's soul.

KREON: Therefore her guards shall pay for their slowness.

126

ANTIGONE: Ah yes, your words tell death to hurry for me.

KREON: I cannot let you hope for any respite.

ANTIGONE: Land of my fathers, O my city, Thebes! O ye gods, eldest of our race!—they hurry me now, they are in haste to have done with me. Behold me, princes of Thebes, the last of the house of your kings—see what I suffer, and by whom—because I feared to forget the fear of heaven!

[*Antigone is led away by the guards, toward the plain.*]

CHORUS:

Even thus in an older day was Danae,
Young and wistful, taken away from the sunlight.
Noble of race was she, in a brass-walled prison
Hid by her father.

Yet the eye of the mighty god beheld her,
Yet to her came Zeus in a golden shower;
Well she bore the seed of the father immortal,
Mothering a hero.

Noble too was that Edonian chieftain,
Rashly who scattered the Bacchanalian fires,
Harried the Maenads, taunted Dionysos,
Angered the Muses:

Him the god made mad, and the godly power
Thrust him, living, deep in a rocky dungeon;
There he learned to know how impious frenzy
Draws divine vengeance.

127

Dire too was the plight of that grieving mother
Who, where the Dark Rocks rise beyond Bosporus,
Far away, in Thracian Salmydessos,
Sacred to Ares,

Saw the fierce implacable wife of Phineos
Strike her children's eyes with the blinding shuttle—
Their little faces turned toward heaven, unseeing,
Tearless and bleeding:

Noble that mother's race, sprung from Erectheos—
Daughter of Boreas she, reared in the wind's caves,
Fleet her foot on the hills; yet upon her too,
Hard bore the Fates.

Dread indeed are the Fates, their ways mysterious:
Neither by wealth nor war—neither by hiding
In strong-walled town, nor fleeing in ships sea-beaten—
Shall man evade them.

[*Teiresias, led by a boy, appears
before the King and the elders.*]

TEIRESIAS: Princes of Thebes, it is a hard journey
for me to come here, for the blind must walk by another's
steps and see with another's eyes; yet I have come.

KREON: And what, Teiresias, are your tidings?

TEIRESIAS: I shall tell you; and listen well to the
seer.

KREON: I have never slighted your counsel.

TEIRESIAS: It is that way you have steered the city
well.

128

KREON: I know, and bear witness, to the worth of your words.

TEIRESIAS: Then mark them now: for I tell you, you stand on fate's thin edge.

KREON: What do you mean? I shudder at your message.

TEIRESIAS: You will know, when you hear the signs my art has disclosed. For lately, as I took my place in my ancient seat of augury, where all the birds of the air gather about me, I heard strange things. They were screaming with feverish rage, their usual clear notes were a frightful jargon; and I knew they were rending each other murderously with their talons: the whirr of their wings told an angry tale.

Straightway, these things filling me with fear, I kindled fire upon an altar, with due ceremony, and laid a sacrifice among the faggots; but Hephaestos would not consume my offering with flame. A moisture oozing out from the bones and flesh trickled upon the embers, making them smoke and sputter. Then the gall burst and scattered on the air, and the steaming thighs lay bared of the fat that had wrapped them.

Such was the failure of the rites by which I vainly asked a sign, as this boy reported them; for his eyes serve me, as I serve others. And I tell you, it is your deeds that have brought a sickness on the State. For the altars of our city and the altars of our hearths have been polluted, one and all, by birds and dogs who have fed on that outraged corpse that was the son of Oedipus. It is for this reason the gods refuse prayer and sacrifice at our hands, and will not consume the meat-offering with flame; nor does any bird give a clear sign by its shrill cry, for they have tasted the fatness of a slain man's blood.

129

Think then on these things, my son. All men are liable to err; but he shows wisdom and earns blessings who heals the ills his errors caused, being not too stubborn; too stiff a will is folly. Yield to the dead, I counsel you, and do not stab the fallen; what prowess is it to slay the slain anew? I have sought your welfare, it is for your good I speak; and it should be a pleasant thing to hear a good counsellor when he counsels for your own gain.

KREON: Old man, you all shoot your shafts at me, like archers at a butt—you too must practise your prophecies on me! Indeed, the tribe of augurs has long trafficked in me and made me their merchandise! Go, seek your price, drive your trade, if you will, in the precious ore of Sardis and the gold of India: but you shall not buy that corpse a grave! No, though the eagles of Zeus should bear their carrion dainties to their Master's throne—no, not even for dread of that will I permit this burial!—for I know that no mortal can pollute the gods. So, hoary prophet, the wisest come to a shameful fall when they clothe shameful counsels in fair words to earn a bribe.

TEIRESIAS: Alas! Does no man know, does none consider. . . .

KREON: What pompous precept now?

TEIRESIAS: . . . that honest counsel is the most priceless gift?

KREON: Yes, and folly the most worthless.

TEIRESIAS: True, and you are infected with that disease.

KREON: This wise man's taunts I shall not answer in kind.

TEIRESIAS: Yet you slander me, saying I augur falsely.

KREON: Well, the tribe of seers always liked money.

130

TEIRESIAS: And the race of tyrants was ever proud and covetous.

KREON: Do you know you are speaking to your king?

TEIRESIAS: I know it: you saved the city when you followed my advice.

KREON: You have your gifts, but you love evil deeds.

TEIRESIAS: Ah, you will sting me to utter the dread secret I have kept hidden in my soul.

KREON: Out with it!—but if you hope to earn a fee by shaking my purpose, you babble in vain.

TEIRESIAS: Indeed I think I shall earn no reward from you.

KREON: Be sure you shall not trade on my resolve.

TEIRESIAS: Know then—aye, know it well!—you will not live through many days, seeing the sun's swift chariot coursing heaven, 'til one whose blood comes from your own heart shall be a corpse, matching two other corpses; because you have given to the shadows one who belongs to the sun, you have lodged a living soul in the grave; yet in this world you detain one who belongs to the world below, a corpse unburied, unhonored and unblest. These things outrage the gods; therefore those dread Erinnyes, who serve the fury of the gods, lie now in wait for you, preparing a vengeance equal to your guilt.

And mark well if I speak these things as a hireling. A time not long delayed will waken the wailing of men and women in your house. But after these cries I hear a more dreadful tumult. For wrath and hatred will stir to arms against you every city whose mangled sons had the burial-rite from dogs and wild beasts, or from birds that will bear the taint of this crime even to the startled hearths of the unburied dead.

Such arrows I do indeed aim at your heart, since you

131

provoke me—they will find their mark, and you shall not escape the sting.—Boy, lead me home, that he may spend his rage on younger men, or learn to curb his bitter tongue and temper his violent mind.

[Teiresias is led away.]

CHORUS: The seer has gone, O King, predicting terrible things. And since the days when my white hair was dark, I know that he has never spoken false auguries for our city.

KREON: I know that too, I know it well, and I am troubled in soul. It is hard to yield; but if by stubbornness I bring my pride to ruin—that too would be hard.

CHORUS: Son of Menoekeos, it is time to heed good counsel.

KREON: What shall I do, then? Speak, and I will obey.

CHORUS: Go free the living maiden from her grave, and make a grave for the unburied dead.

KREON: Is this indeed your counsel? Do you bid me yield?

CHORUS: Yes, and without delay; for the swift judgments of the gods cut short the folly of men.

KREON: It is hard to do—to retreat from a firm stand—but I yield, I will obey you. We must not wage a vain war with Fate.

CHORUS: Go then, let your own hand do these things; do not leave them to others.

KREON: Even as I am I will go: come, servants, all of you, bring tools to raise one grave and open another. Since our judgment has taken this turn, I who buried the girl will free her myself.—My heart misgives me, it is best to keep the established laws, even to life's end.

132

[*Kreon and his servants go
toward the plain.*]

CHORUS:

O god of many names,
Fruit of the daughter of Kadmos
Whom the loud-thundering Zeus
Embraced amid lightnings,

Ever your praise be sung
From famed Italia's vineyards
To the Eleusinian vale
Where Deo welcomes all;
But most, O Bacchos,
In Thebes where you dwell,
In Thebes, mother of Bacchants,
And by that stream Ismenus
Where the dragon's teeth were sown!

Where the two slender peaks
Of Muse-haunted Parnassos
Rise against the sky,
The torch-flames have revealed you;
And you have been seen
Where the Corycian nymphs
Dance for joy of you
Through the flowering meadows
Beside Castalia's stream.

But from Nysa's hills,
With twining ivy mantled,
And from many a headland
Green with clustered vines,

Even while your name is lifted
In all men's song and prayer,
You turn to the dragon's land
And visit the ways of Thebes.

Thebes, where your mother
Conceived amid lightning,
First among cities
Stand always in your grace.
And now when the people
By this new plague are stricken,
Swiftly from Parnassos
You come with healing tread!

O god with whom the stars,
The stars whose breath is fire,
Rejoice as they move in heaven—
O lord of the hymns of the night,
O Kadmean son of Zeus,
Amid the dancing maidens
Appear to us in majesty—
O giver of all good gifts,
Iacchos, heed our prayer!

[*A Messenger appears, from
the direction of the plain.*]

MESSENGER: Neighbors of the house of Kadmos,
dwellers within Amphion's walls, there is no state of mortal
life that I would praise or pity, for none is beyond swift
change. Fortune raises men up and fortune casts them
down from day to day, and no man can foretell the fate
of things established. For Kreon was blest in all that I
count happiness: he had honor as our savior; power as
134

our king; pride as the father of princely children. Now all is ended. For when a man is stripped of happiness, I count him not with the living—he is but a breathing corpse. Let a man have riches heaped in his house, and live in royal splendor; yet I would not give the shadow of a breath for all, if they bring no gladness.

CHORUS: What fearful news have you about our princes?

MESSENGER: Death; and the living are guilty of the dead.

CHORUS: Who is the slayer—who is the slain?

MESSENGER: Haemon has perished, and it was no stranger shed his blood.

CHORUS: His father's hand, or his own?

MESSENGER: His own, maddened by his father's crime.

CHORUS: O prophet, how true your word has proved!

MESSENGER: This is the way things are: consider then, how to act.

CHORUS: Look!—the unhappy Eurydike, Kreon's consort, comes from the house; is it by chance, or has she heard these tidings of her son?

[*Eurydike comes from the house.*]

EURYDIKE: I heard your words, citizens, as I was going to the shrine of Pallas with my prayers. As I loosed the bolts of the gate, the message of woe to my household smote my ear. I sank back, stricken with horror, into the arms of my handmaids, and my senses left me. Yet say again these tidings. I shall hear them as one who is no stranger to grief.

MESSENGER: Dear lady, I will tell you what I saw, I will hide nothing of the truth. I would gladly tell you a

135

happier tale, but it would soon be found out false. Truth is the only way.—I guided your lord the King to the furthest part of the plain, where the body of Polyneikes, torn by dogs, still lay unpitied. There we prayed to the goddess of the roads, and to Pluto, in mercy to restrain their wrath. We washed the dead with holy rites, and all that was left of the mortal man we burned with fresh-plucked branches; and over the ashes at last we raised a mound of his native earth.

That done, we turned our steps toward those fearsome caves where in a cold nuptial chamber, with couch of stone, that maiden had been given as a bride to Death. But from afar off, one of us heard a voice wailing aloud, and turned to tell our master Kreon.

And as the King drew nearer, the sharp anguish of broken cries came to his ears. Then he groaned and said like one in pain, "Can my sudden fear be true? Am I on the saddest road I ever went? That voice is my son's! Hurry, my servants, to the tomb, and through the gap where the stones have been torn out, look into the cell— tell me if it is Haemon's voice I hear, or if my wits are tortured by the gods."

At these words from our stricken master, we went to make that search; and in the dim furthest part of the tomb we saw Antigone hanging by the neck, her scarf of fine linen twisted into a cruel noose. And there too we saw Haemon—his arms about her waist, while he cried out upon the loss of his bride, and his father's deed, and his ill-starred love.

But now the King approached, and saw him, and cried out with horror, and went in and called with piteous voice, "Unhappy boy, what a deed have you done, breaking into this tomb! What purpose have you? Has grief stolen

136

your reason? Come forth, my son! I pray you—I implore!"
The boy answered no word, but glared at him with fierce
eyes, spat in his face, and drew his cross-hilted sword.
His father turned and fled, and the blow missed its mark.
Then that maddened boy, torn between grief and rage and
penitence, straightway leaned upon his sword, and drove
it half its length into his side; and in the little moment
before death, he clasped the maiden in his arms, and her
pale cheek was red where his blood gushed forth.

Corpse enfolding corpse they lie; he has won his bride,
poor lad, not here but in the halls of Death; to all of us
he has left a terrible witness that man's worst error is to
reject good counsel.

[*Eurydike goes into the house.*]

CHORUS: What does this mean? The lady turns and
goes without a word.

MESSENGER: I too am startled; but I think it means
she is too proud to cry out before the people. Within the
house, with her handmaids about her, the tears will flow.
Life has taught her prudence.

CHORUS: It may be; yet I fear. To me such silence
seems more ominous than many lamentations.

MESSENGER: Then I will go into the house, and learn
if some tragic purpose has formed in her tortured heart.
Yes, you speak wisely; too much silence may hide terrible
meanings.

[*The Messenger enters the house. As he
goes, Kreon comes into the open place
before the house with attendants carrying
the shrouded body of Haemon on a bier.*]

CHORUS: See, the King himself draws near, with the

137

sad proof of his folly; this tells a tale of no violence by strangers, but—if I may say it—of his own misdeeds.

KREON: Woe for the sins of a darkened soul, the sins of a stubborn pride that played with death! Behold me, the father who has slain, behold the son who has perished! I am punished for the blindness of my counsels. Alas my son, cut down in youth untimely, woe is me!—your spirit fled—not yours the fault and folly, but my own!

CHORUS: Too late, too late your eyes are opened!

KREON: I have learned that bitter lesson. But it was some god, I think, darkened my mind and turned me into ways of cruelty. Now my days are overthrown and my joys trampled. Alas, man's labors come but to foolish ends!

[The Messenger comes from the house.]

MESSENGER: Sire, one sees your hands are not empty, but there is more laid up in store for you. Woeful is the burden you bear, and you must look on further woes within your house.

KREON: Why, how can there be more?

MESSENGER: Your queen is dead, the mother of that lad—unhappy lady! This is Fate's latest blow.

KREON: Death, Death, how many deaths will stay your hunger? For me is there no mercy? O messenger of evil, bearer of bitter tidings, what is this you tell me? I was already dead, but you smite me anew. What do you say?—what is this news you bring of slaughter heaped on slaughter?

[The doors of the King's house are opened, and the corpse of Eurydike is disclosed.]

CHORUS: Behold with your own eyes!

138

KREON: Oh, horror!—woe upon woe! Can any further dreadful thing await me? I have but now raised my son in these arms—and here again I see a corpse before me. Alas, unhappy mother—alas, alas my child!

MESSENGER: At the altar of your house, self-stabbed with a keen knife, she suffered her darkening eyes to close, while she lamented that other son, Megareus, who died so nobly but a while ago, and then this boy whose corpse is here beside you. But with her last breath and with a bitter cry she invoked evil upon you, the slayer of your sons.

KREON: Will no one strike me to the heart with the two-edged sword?—miserable that I am, and plunged in misery!

MESSENGER: Yes, both this son's death and that other son's, were charged to you by her whose corpse you see.

KREON: But how did she do this violence upon herself?

MESSENGER: Her own hand struck her to the heart, when she had heard how this boy died.

KREON: I cannot escape the guilt of these things, it rests on no other of mortal kind. I, only I, am the slayer, wretched that I am—I own the truth. Lead me away, my servants, lead me quickly hence, for my life is but death.

CHORUS: You speak well, if any speech is good amid so much evil. When all is trouble, the briefest way is best.

KREON: Oh let it come now, the fate most merciful for me, my last day—that will be the best fate of all. Oh let it come swiftly, that I may not look upon tomorrow's light!

CHORUS: That is hidden in the future. Present tasks claim our care. The ordering of the future does not rest with mortals.

KREON: Yet all my desire is summed up in that prayer.

139

CHORUS: Pray no more: no man evades his destiny.

KREON: Lead me away, I pray you; a rash, foolish man, who has slain you, O my son, unwittingly, and you too, my wife—unhappy that I am! Where can I find comfort, where can I turn my gaze?—for where I have turned my hand, all has gone wrong; and this last blow breaks me and bows my head.

[*Kreon is led into his house
as the Chorus speaks.*]

CHORUS:

If any man would be happy, and not broken by Fate,
Wisdom is the thing he should seek, for happiness hides
    there.
Let him revere the gods and keep their words inviolate,
For proud men who speak great words come in the end to
    despair,
And learn wisdom in sorrow, when it is too late.